THE BOOK OF JOB

STUDIES IN BIBLICAL THEOLOGY

A series of monographs designed to provide clergy and laymen with the best work in biblical scholarship both in this country and abroad

Advisory Editors:

STUDIES IN BIBLICAL THEOLOGY

Second Series · 11

THE BOOK OF JOB

Its Origin and Purpose

NORMAN H. SNAITH

SCM PRESS LTD
BLOOMSBURY STREET LONDON

334 00791 7

First published 1968
Second impression 1972

© SCM Press Ltd 1968

Reproduced and Printed in Great Britain by
Redwood Press Limited
Trowbridge & London

CONTENTS

PREFACE

THIS book is developed from lectures delivered in the University of Oxford in 1963-4 when I was Speaker's Lecturer in Biblical Studies. I am grateful for the opportunity which this appointment afforded me of bringing into some sort of coherence thoughts concerning the Book of Job which have been gradually developed during half a lifetime.

The point of view here taken concerning the problem of the Book of Job is that substantially the whole book is the work of one man. He is responsible for the present form of both prologue and epilogue. He is the author of the speeches of Job and the three friends. He is responsible for the Elihu speeches and for both Yahweh speeches. Further, I do not think that the author was primarily concerned with the problem of suffering, whether suffering in general or the suffering of one particular individual. His main problem is the problem of the transcendent God. Has this God anything at all to do with this world of men and their affairs? How can mortal man ever get into touch with this High God? How can the High God ever be imminently concerned with the affairs of men?

This problem of the High God is discussed against the background of the sufferings of Job. Here is the author's example of the incidence of the problem: human suffering in this world, and the blatant injustice of so much of it. But it is not the basic problem of the book. The basic problem is the basic problem of religion the whole world over. Most of all it is the problem of monotheism. To use phraseology associated with the study of primitive religions: how can the High God fulfil the functions of the low gods, and still remain a High God? The answer of the Book of Job is submission: God still far away, unapproachable and incomprehensible, but with a working rule for men. This working rule is: the fear of the Lord, and turning aside from evil (Job 28.28). This, as Charles Wesley wrote, is 'our business here below'. Orthodox Christianity has sought to solve the problem by saying both Yes and No. God is indeed a High God, but the

vii

incarnation has brought God near to man (made him imminent) and the Holy Spirit can indeed indwell men (made him immanent in man).

I have been anticipated in part in some of my conclusions concerning the authorship and constitution of the Book of Job by Robert Gordis of the Jewish Theological Seminary in New York City. So far as the authenticity of the Elihu speeches is concerned, Rabbi Gordis's work is to be found in 'Elihu the Intruder', *Biblical and Other Studies*, ed. Alexander Altmann (1963), pp. 60-78. For Rabbi Gordis's attitude to the Book of Job as a whole, see his *The Book of God and Man; A Study of Job* (1965). My earlier views have undergone little or no modification because of Rabbi Gordis's published works, but since I have read Rabbi Gordis's book, I have rewritten most of what I had already done. He and I have backgrounds that are wholly different and we have studied the Book of Job from widely different attitudes, but we agree in a substantial number of details.

The titles of works of commentators cited in the text can be obtained from the lists given by E. Dhorme (*A Commentary on the Book of Job*, ET, 1967, pp. v-vi), C. Cohen (*Interpreter's Dictionary of the Bible*, II, 1962, pp. 924-5) and O. Eissfeldt (*The Old Testament, An Introduction*, ET, 1956, p. 764).

ABBREVIATIONS

ANET	*Ancient Near Eastern Texts relating to the Old Testament* ed. J. B. Pritchard, 2nd ed. 1955
Aq	Aquila
AV	Authorized Version (King James Version)
AVm	Authorized Version (margin)
BDB	*A Hebrew and English Lexicon of the Old Testament*, ed. Francis Brown, with the co-operation of S. R. Drive and C. A. Briggs, 1906
Codices	
A	Alexandrinus
B	Vaticanus
C	Ephraemi rescriptus
Sin	Sinaiticus
CR	*Contemporary Review*
DOTT	*Documents from the Old Testament Times*, ed. D. Winton Thomas, 1958
DV	Douay-Rheims Version
EVV	English Versions
GK	W. Gesenius, *Hebrew Grammar*, ed. and enl. E. Kautzsch 2nd English ed. 1910
IB	*Interpreter's Bible*
ICC	International Critical Commentary
JB	Jerusalem Bible
Ker	Kerithoth (Mishnah)
LXX	Septuagint
MT	Masoretic (Hebrew) Text
NEB	New English Bible
RSV	Revised Standard Version
RV	Revised Version
RVm	Revised Version (margin)
S	Syriac (*Peshiṭta*) Version
Sym	Symmachus
T	Targum
Th	Theodotion

Ugarit
    A   Aqhat
    B   Baal
    B.Fr   Baal (fragments)
    H   Hadad
    K   Keret
V   Vulgate
VT   *Vetus Testamentum*
VTS   Supplement to Vetus Testamentum
ZAW   *Zeitschrift für die alttestamentliche Wissenschaft*

I

THE FOLK-TALE AND THE ORIGINAL BOOK

1. *The Original Book*

THE Book of Job is found in the third section of the Hebrew Bible, in the *Kethubim*, the Writings. Its actual position varies. According to the Talmud tradition (*Baba bathra* 14b), it comes third and follows Ruth and Psalms. The main Sephardi (Spanish) tradition also makes it third, but following Chronicles and Psalms. It is third also in the Ashkenazi (mid-European) tradition, where it follows Psalms and Proverbs. This is the order usually followed in printed editions of the Hebrew Bible, though not in the third edition of Kittel's *Biblica Hebraica* (text by Paul Kahle), where the order of the Leningrad Codex B 19a is followed, with Job second and Proverbs third. The consistent element throughout is that Job is linked with the other two poetical books, so that Psalms, Job and Proverbs come together. Jerome's list of the books of the Hagiographa (Writings) begins with Job (*Prolog. Gal.*), and he follows this with 'David' and 'Solomon', that is, Psalms and Proverbs, presumably because he is following the LXX tradition which fits the various books into what was believed to be the proper historical order, it being presumed that Job lived before David.[1]

The English versions have followed what, by the thirteenth century, had become the accepted order in the Vulgate, with the Protestant versions omitting the books of the Apocrypha, while the Roman Catholic versions retain them. Thus Job follows the historical books, and precedes Psalms and Proverbs. As we have indicated, this is because Job was reckoned to have lived before David. The Syriac (*Peshiṭta*) version is much more radical. It re-

[1] Further details and some variations from the normal patterns are to be found in H. E. Ryle, *The Canon of the Old Testament*, 2nd ed., 1895, pp. 210-38, 281f.; in H. B. Swete, *An Introduction to the Old Testament in Greek*, 1900, pp. 197-230; and in C. D. Ginsburg, *Introduction to the Massoretico-critical edition of the Hebrew Bible*, reissued 1966, pp. 1-8.

I

gards Job as having lived in the patriarchal age, and therefore it places the book immediately after Deuteronomy. This actually was placing the book as early as possible, since no zeal for the historical order would induce any translator or editor, of the Greek, Latin or Syriac, to disturb the priority of or interfere with the order of the first 'Five Books of Moses'. The Talmud (*Baba Bathra* 14b) recognized this: 'If it be said, Job lived in the days of Moses, Job therefore should be placed at the head.' The reason given against this procedure was, 'verily, we do not begin with calamity', but doubtless the true reason was that nothing could be permitted to disturb the priority of the Torah.[2]

The pattern and the story of the Book of Job are well known. The book consists of a prologue and an epilogue, both in prose, and within these a series of speeches, all in verse, except for the short introduction to the speeches of Elihu (32.1-5). In the prologue Job appears as a wealthy desert sheik, blessed with sons and daughters, and having all his wealth in sheep and goats, camels, cattle and she-asses.[3] Job's family live a life which involves a regular round of feasting; seven sons and seven days, one day at each son's establishment successively. They are the true aristocrats of the desert and live in desert luxury. Job himself is truly and strictly pious, 'perfect and upright', and he goes to every length to avoid all offence in the sight of God. So much for the first scene of the prologue.

The second scene opens with God holding his heavenly court. All the heavenly beings are present in attendance on him, including the Satan, that servant of God whose particular duty it is to test men to see how far their performance matches their profession. When the Satan had developed in Jewish thought into the enemy of God and the prince of the counter-kingdom of evil,[4] this role of inspectorship was allocated to the prophet Elijah. But already by the time the prologue of the Book of Job was written, the Satan has become more than a little cynical, so that when God

[2] Modern printed Syriac Bibles follow the order of English Bibles, with the Trinitarian Bible Society edition and the Urmia 1852 edition omitting the Apocrypha, and the 1886-91 Mosul (Dominican) edition retaining it.

[3] We translate *ṣ'ōn* in 1.3 as 'sheep and goats', since the flock of ancient times, as now in the Near East and India, consisted of sheep and goats, distinguishable at a distance only by tails down or tails up.

[4] Eph. 2.2: 'The prince of the power of the air (AV, RV, RSV); 'The commander of the spiritual powers of the air' (NEB).

declares that Job is perfect and upright, the Satan takes leave to cast doubts on Job's integrity and disinterested piety. He claims that Job serves God because it pays him to do so. Any man in his senses would do what is right and would be as scrupulous about it as Job is, if he was sure that thus he could be certain of divine protection and great prosperity and comfort. So the Satan receives authority to afflict Job, and in a series of catastrophes Job is stripped of all his possessions, his beasts and all his property, all his servants, all his sons. But still Job does not sin, nor does he charge God with unfair, unworthy conduct.

The third scene is once more the heavenly court, but later. Once more God proudly declares Job's disinterested piety. Job has passed all the tests which God has permitted the Satan to impose. But the Satan still doubts, and ultimately he receives permission to inflict upon Job every and any kind of physical distress short of death. Job is therefore smitten with a painful, unsightly skin disease, so that he becomes outcast in pain and degradation. He sits on the ash-heap outside the city (LXX: 2.8), where all the mendicants and especially the outcasts are to be found. But still Job utters no sinful word, and he continues to endure without complaint all his misfortunes in spite of all that his wife says— and according to LXX she has a very great deal indeed to say.

Then (2.11) three friends arrive, Eliphaz the Temanite, Bildad the Shuhite and Zophar the Naamathite. They sit in silence for seven long days and never say a word. Thus ends the prologue.

With ch. 3 there begins a series of speeches, all in verse and consisting of two complete cycles of six speeches each, plus what is usually said to be the remnants of a third cycle. Job makes a speech, and this is followed by a speech from Eliphaz. Job makes a second speech, and this is followed by a speech from Bildad. Job makes a third speech, and this is followed by a speech from Zophar. This completes the first cycle and brings us to the end of ch. 12. The second cycle has the same pattern of speech and counter-speech, and so we come to the end of ch. 21. The so-called third cycle begins with ch. 22, but Bildad's speech is very short indeed, and there is no speech at all from Zophar. Instead of following the previous pattern Job makes what seem to be two third-speeches: ch. 28, the poem on wisdom, appears as a continuation of ch. 27, and this is followed by a long speech from Job, consisting of three chapters, 29-31. At ch. 32 a new character appears and he is introduced by a short prose passage. He is Elihu, the angry young man, and he speaks at great length. He makes four speeches, one after the other, and these comprise chs. 32-37. In ch. 38, God himself intervenes and speaks to Job out of the storm. God takes no notice of the three friends and no notice of Elihu. He speaks to Job and to Job alone. There are two speeches from God, and two short replies by Job. This brings us to the end of the verse section at 42.6. Job abhors himself and repents in sackcloth and ashes.

The book concludes with an epilogue. The three friends are pardoned through Job's intercessory prayer on their behalf, though it is by no means clear what their offence has been. It is said (42.7f.) that the friends have not spoken about God the things that are right, as Job has done. This is a surprising statement, since the three friends have been thoroughly orthodox. If any man has transgressed the limits of what it is proper to say about God, it is Job. There are times when he has gone as near to accusing God of unjust and irresponsible behaviour as any man can well go. Perhaps the author is writing from his own point of view, which is that the old orthodoxy is unsound, and can be bolstered up only by twisting the facts. Job has truly faced the facts. However, all ends well. The three friends are pardoned. Job's fortunes are changed. He receives twice as much as he had before. This brings us to 42.10. But now the story starts up again. All his brothers and sisters and all his former acquaintances—we have heard nothing of them before—come, show him sympathy and comfort. They each give him a coin and a gold ring. Job ends with seven (? fourteen) sons and three daughters,[5] and for some

---

[5] Did Job have seven or fourteen sons as well as the three daughters in the days of his restoration? In 42.13 the Hebrew has the word *šib'ānā*. This form is strange, and *GK* 97*c* refers to Ewald's explanation that it is 'an old feminine substantive' (*ein Sieband*, a set of seven), but says that it is more likely to be a scribal error. Many commentators emend to the normal *šib'ā* (seven) without more ado, as eleven de Rossi MSS have done. It is more likely that the form is a conflation of *šib'ān* (twice-seven: E. Dhorme, *A Commentary on Job*, ET, 1967, p. 651) and *šib'ā* (seven). It could be an archaic form (G. Fohrer, *Studien zum BucheHiob*, 1963, p. 431). The Talmud understood the word to mean 'twice-seven'. Cf. also I Chron. 25.5, where Heman's fourteen sons and three daughters are evidence of his great prosperity. This could well be. Double prosperity could mean double the number of sons even more markedly than double the number of domesticated animals. Doubling the number of daughters is no particular benefit. The most the author could do for them was to say that they were the most beautiful in all the land and that they were

reason the three daughters are mentioned by name. Job receives twice as much property (sheep, camels, oxen, she-asses) as he had originally. And he lives to be a hundred and forty years old, twice the allotted span of Ps. 90.10.[6]

The epilogue, as it stands at present, assumes the existence of a speech by God, speeches by Job and speeches by the three friends. There is no reference to Elihu, and much has been made of this. The most likely explanation is that the Elihu speeches were introduced into the book after the epilogue had reached its present form. This does not, however, necessarily involve that they are the work of another author.

But this is by no means the end of the problems set by the epilogue. There is the difficulty already mentioned, the statement in 42.7f. that the three friends had maligned God, whereas Job had spoken correctly of him. We do not find this statement as difficult as most writers find it, since we see in it the author's own condemnation of the facile orthodoxy of the three friends and his commendation of the attitude of Job who at least has had the courage to look the facts of human life in the face. We do not agree that there must have been some dislocation or some substitution or some addition somewhere in order to account for this

wealthy in their own right. Daughters are not sons, and it was having many sons that was the sign of divine blessing. It may be that the naming of the daughters is an additional item of prestige.

It may well be that the three daughters survived the catastrophe of 1.18f. The Hebrew does not say clearly that the three daughters died. It has $ne^\varsigma\bar{a}rim$ (young men) in all four lists of casualties: vv. 15, 16, 17 and 19. In vv. 15, 16, and 17 the reference is to Job's employees, his servants, with specific reference in v. 16 to the shepherds, as LXX and S have seen (probably) interpreting. AV and RV have 'young men' in v. 19, this means the seven sons; but RSV and JB have 'the young people', which means both sons and daughters. It is plain that the reference in v. 19 is to some, at least, of Job's children. LXX inserts 'your'; V has *liberos* (children), S has *ṭlāyē*, which strictly refers to youngsters under seven years old.

[6] In any event, Job lived to a very great age: he saw the fourth generation, not only sons' sons, but sons' sons' sons, and he died 'old and full of days'. How long he lived is uncertain. The Hebrew has $'ah^a r\bar{e}-z\bar{o}'t$, found only here and Ezra 9.10; also with 'all' in II Chron. 21.18; 35.20. The phrase is late and was interpreted both by LXX and V to mean 'after the time of Job's trouble' (LXX 'after the plague'; V *post haec*). LXX says it involves 170 years more, making a total of 240 (first corrector of Codex Sin; Codices A and C add another 8, i.e. 248 in all). S follows the Hebrew. EVV leave it to be assumed that Job lived for another 140 years, making 210 years in all, but JB definitely makes it 140 years in all. This involves assuming that the Hebrew phrase $'ah^a r\bar{e}-z\bar{o}'t$ is a transitional phrase and has lost its definite time-point just as the phrase $'ah^a r\bar{e}-k\bar{e}n$ did.

statement in 42.7. Alt[7] emphasized rightly that 42.7-10 does not go with 42.11-17. He found two stories in the prologue and epilogue: ch. 1; 42.11-17 and ch. 2; 42.7-10, and he holds that in the latter story the three friends must have urged Job to curse God, this being the explanation of 42.8. Gordis[8] rightly says that this theory will not do. There is too much missing in both stories; it is Job's wife who urged him to curse God (2.9); to say 'what is not right' (*lō' nᵉkōhā*) about God is not necessarily to curse him. Gordis then goes on to point out that 42.10 and 42.11 do not fit together.[9] The sudden disappearance of the three friends together with the equally sudden appearance of a whole host of relations and friends is strange. It is the first time we have heard of these people, and they come with the same intention as the three friends—to commiserate with and to comfort Job. As it turns out, they come to join in a thanksgiving party for Job's restoration to a good, and an even better fortune.

Another curious element in these verses is the use of the phrase 'lift up the face' (vv. 8f.). This phrase has various shades of meaning. It can mean 'grant a request' (Gen. 19.21; I Sam. 25.35). It can also mean 'receive with honour', 'receive (back) into favour' (Gen. 32.20 [MT 21]; Mal. 1.8f.; II Kings 5.1). We have both usages in these verses. In v. 8 the meaning is that God will grant Job's request on behalf of the three friends. In v. 9 the meaning is that God will receive Job back into favour. This explanation makes good sense of both passages, and it fits in with the theory that there are two separate stories in the epilogue. This we believe to be the case, as Alt and others have seen. All this has nothing at all to do with Elihu and his speeches. If Elihu and his speeches had never existed, it would still be true that there are two distinct stories in the epilogue. Our solution is that there was originally a prologue and an epilogue which did not contain the three friends.

Suppose the prologue originally ended at 2.10. This involves the omission of the last three verses, and it is a straight, plain, clean cut. Now turn to the epilogue. Suppose that this originally began with the last phrase of 42.9: 'and the Lord accepted Job', which means that after Job had repented in sackcloth and ashes

[7] 'Zur Vorgeschichte des Buches Hiob', *ZAW* 55 (1937), pp. 265-8.
[8] *The Book of God and Man: A Study of Job*, 1965, p. 72.
[9] *ibid.*, pp. 74f.

(42.6) God received him back into favour and more than restored his fortunes—doubled them, in fact.[10] Then there is the curiously misplaced clause in v. 10: 'when he prayed for his friend (*sic*)'. The difficulty of the phrase is disguised in the English versions, in RSV as well as in AV and RV. It is a very strange clause. The syntax is unusual and it interrupts the sense of the verse. In any case, why should God accept Job and restore his fortunes when he prayed for his friend? Surely it ought to have been either that Job prayed for the friends and their fortunes were enhanced or that the friends prayed for Job and his fortunes were changed. LXX has seen this difficulty and says that when Job prayed for the friends, God forgave them their sin. But why does the verse say 'his friend'?[11] Without this curious and curiously placed clause, we have in v. 10 a perfect sequence: 'Then the Lord accepted Job, and the Lord restored the fortunes of Job, and the Lord gave Job twice as much as he had before.' Our explanation of the phrase is that it was inserted when (or after) the present first three verses were added at the beginning of the epilogue, in an attempt to reconcile the conflicting statements.

If we omit the three friends and all that they say, all that Job says in reply to them, together with Elihu and all that he says, and also ch. 28, then we are left with chs. 3; 29-31, the Yahweh speeches (38-39; 40.6-41.26), and an apology (40.3-5) and re-cantation (42.1-6) by Job. All this is included within a prologue and an epilogue, both in prose, the present prologue shortened by the last three verses, and the present epilogue shortened by the first three verses (but including the last phrase of 42.9 and omitting the strange, interpolated phrase in 42.10). This all makes a coherent story, and there is no need to assume any variation from straight cuts, apart from the one phrase in 42.10.

To reiterate: the first edition of the Book of Job as it was first shaped by the author consisted of 1.1-2.10; 3 and 29-31, 38-39 and an apology by Job (40.3-5), 40.6-41.26, parts of 42.1-6, then

---

[10] The phrase *šûb šᵉbût* means 'turn a turning', i.e. change the fortunes; so Ewald and all since; cf. RSV.

[11] The Hebrew definitely has the singular. According to *GK* 91*k*, this singular may be 'a collective singular', a suggestion which looks too much like the last despairing gasp of the dying. The other two examples cited in *BDB* are II Sam. 30.26, where the text is uncertain, and Prov. 29.18, which is an error. The 'etc.' of *BDB* 946*a* is decidedly optimistic, to say the least.

42.9*d* ('and the Lord accepted Job') and 42.10-17, but omitting the phrase 'when he prayed for his friend'.

This proposed solution is in part similar to that proposed by Robert Gordis.[12] He thinks that the author took the traditional folk-tale for his own purposes and that he added to the original material 'two brief jointures', 2.11-13 and 42.7-10. This means, as we understand Rabbi Gordis, that in his opinion the three friends were not in the original folk-tale, but were introduced by the author when he first wrote the book. We agree that the three friends were not in the original folk-tale, but we are of the opinion that they were not in our author's first draft. We think that the first draft follows the pattern of the so-called 'The Babylonian Job' or some wisdom writing closely similar to it (see below, pp. 19-23), a writing with a long soliloquy and an intervention by the god. Later, the author had other thoughts, and into his first edition he interpolated the three friends and the dialogue, making suitable additions to the prologue and to the epilogue. Also, either at this time or, more likely, still later, he introduced Elihu, and it is in these Elihu speeches that we get the author's final thoughts about his subject—the problem of communication between the High God and the world which he has made.

Before we turn to consider the origin of the prologue and the epilogue and what the author of the Book of Job did with them, there are three other matters to be considered.

First: the so-called dialogue between Job and the three friends is scarcely a dialogue in any normal sense of the word. Even the more formal speeches in the Greek tragedies are more closely interrelated than these. In the Book of Job we have a dialogue only in the sense that they all speak in turn, one after the other, with Job speaking after every speech by one of the friends. The content of each speech is usually strangely independent of what has gone before and what follows. Virtually, any one speech could be omitted and it never would be missed. The speech-makers are like the protagonist in an argument who does indeed condescend from time to time to allow his opponent to say something, but when he speaks again (which he does at the slenderest opportunity), he does not reply, but mostly ignores it all and continues

[12] *The Book of God and Man*, p. 73.

from where he himself left off. The independence of the speeches is plain and is generally recognized. Notably is this so in ch. 28. Practically all scholars, especially those of recent date, are agreed that this chapter is a distinct piece. They say that it was introduced later, perhaps by another author, perhaps by the original author himself, but certainly as a distinct and separate piece. But this independence seems to be everywhere. Everything in the book is formally united, but strangely detached: juxtaposition everywhere, but very little unity anywhere.

Second: it is a curious feature that in the earlier parts of the dialogue Job's speeches tend to be approximately twice as long as the speech of the friend who has immediately preceded him. Our suggestion is that perhaps the author's general pattern for the dialogue was (1) speech by Job, speech by Eliphaz, speech by Job; (2) speech by Job, speech by Bildad, speech by Job; (3) speech by Job, speech by Zophar, speech by Job. The soundness of this conjecture can be neither proved nor disproved, because of the independence and isolation of the speeches. It would work out as follows:

The first cycle opens with ch. 3, the author having made use of a chapter which belonged to his original scheme, this chapter having been originally the opening of Job's soliloquy (chs. 3; 29-31). Eliphaz, as the first and the leader of the three friends, breaks in on Job's soliloquy, and this has the effect of making ch. 3 the opening speech of the dialogue. Its length is approximately that of a normal speech of the three friends, and half the usual length of a speech by Job, as these speeches are commonly reckoned. Instead of considering the whole of chs. 6 and 7 to be Job's reply to Eliphaz, it is better to take ch. 6 as Job's reply to him. This is virtually what 6.1 says and infers: 'Then Job answered and said'. Thus ch. 6 ends the first phase of the first cycle of speeches. The second phase begins with a speech by Job comprising ch. 7 and continues with a speech by Bildad in ch. 8 and a reply by Job in ch. 9: note again 9.1. The third phase then would be: speech by Job in ch. 10, speech by Zophar in ch. 11, and a reply by Job in chs. 12 and 13. This ends the first cycle. It is possible that the first cycle ends with ch. 12.[13]

---

[13] The 'this' of EVV in 13.1 is not in the Hebrew text. On the other hand, EVV are here following V (AV quite often throughout tends to be influenced by V), and here is actually a conflation of the Hebrew 'all' and LXX 'these things'.

We think that the second cycle begins with 14.1 because Job starts once more with the topic of the incidence of suffering. This he does in 3.3; 7.1; 10.1; and also in 17.1. The usual disunity of the speeches and indeed disunity within the speeches makes anything like certainty impossible, but at any rate we have given to such verses as 6.1 their natural and proper meaning.[14] The second phase of the second cycle begins with a speech by Job in ch. 17, and it continues with a reply by Bildad in ch. 18 and a reply by Job beginning at 19.1 (compare this verse with 18.1). It is hereabouts that the phase-pattern begins to falter, just as it is hereabouts that the cycle-pattern shows the first signs of breaking down. We take the ending of Job's reply to Bildad to be 19.22. This is the end of the second phase of the second cycle. The third phase would then begin with 19.23, a short speech by Job. Zophar's reply begins at 20.1, and Job's reply begins at 21.1. We take this reply of Job's to end at 21.21, so that the so-called third cycle begins with 21.22, a speech by Job. Eliphaz's reply is in ch. 22 and Job's reply to Eliphaz is in ch. 23. But at ch. 24 the whole scheme of the dialogue breaks down entirely,[15] and we have separate, independent pieces from 24.1 to the end of ch. 28.

Third: The suggestion that the author should make an addition to his first work is not as wholly revolutionary as some may suppose. The possibility has been admitted already by those who think that the Elihu speeches are a later addition by the same author. Our suggestion goes one stage further than this. We propose three editions of the book: (1) the shortened prologue plus the shortened epilogue (i.e. without the three friends), Job's soliloquy, Yahweh's replies with an apology and a submission by Job; (2) the present prologue, the present epilogue, the three friends, the miscellaneous pieces in chs. 24-28 and all the poetic pieces of the first edition; (3) the book as it now stands, with the Elihu speeches inserted at the end of the dialogue after all the humans have finished speaking, but, as one would expect, before the divine speeches of chs. 38-41. With this, compare F. J. Bailey's *Festus* in all its successive editions from the author's youth to his old age. Another instance is Bulwer Lytton's *Zacci*, which he later rewrote in part, altered the order of some of the chapters, thus

---

[14] See also A. and M. Hanson, *The Book of Job*, Torch Bible Commentaries, 1953, p. 13.
[15] See below, pp. 58-63.

varying the plot, and then published under the title *Zanoni*. Rudyard Kipling altered the end of *The Light that Failed*, but, as he himself might say, 'that is another story'.

2. *The Folk-tale*

Was there ever such a person as Job?

There was apparently a tradition concerning a man named Job. He was one of three righteous men: Noah, Daniel and Job (Ezek. 14.14, 20). Where did Ezekiel learn that these three men were righteous? So far as Noah is concerned, the answer may well be Gen. 6.9: 'Noah was a righteous man', but this sentence is from the Priestly tradition. It is generally agreed that the Priestly tradition reached its final form not later than, say, c. 400 B.C., though some scholars make the date somewhat earlier. The tradition may have come through the Priestly document (but this is difficult, since presumably Ezek. 14 is earlier than the Priestly document, whatever its precise date may be) or it may be much earlier and quite ancient. But where would the author of Ezek. 14 find that Daniel or Job was righteous? Even if we assume, which is unlikely, that Ezek. 14 is later than the Book of Job, we still are left with the beginnings of the Daniel tradition. There is indeed an ancient tradition of one *Dan'el*, which is the actual spelling of the name in Ezek. 14.14, 20, and this is found also in Ugarit in the legend of the birth and fate of Aqhat. King Dan'el is a king who judges righteously (*Aqhat* V 8.9: He judges the case of the widow: adjudicates the cause of the fatherless), and incidentally in the Ugarit text there are references to two different series of seven successive days of offerings and sacred meals (*Aqhat* II 1.1-12; II 2.32-40). The spelling of the name in the book of Daniel is different. There the spelling is *Dāniyyēl*, and the Masoretes 'read' this in Ezek. 14.14, 20, and also in Ezek. 28.3, where *Dan'el* is the traditional wise man of ancient time and legend.[16] Thus, certainly for Daniel and most likely for Job also, the suggestion of a *Volksbuch* (D. B. Macdonald and B. Duhm) is the most fruitful suggestion of all, and it has been mightily supported by the actual finding of some elements of such a tradition in ancient Ugarit.

There are many elements in both prologue and epilogue which show all the characteristics of a folk-tale. It is not, however, easy

[16] This verse is probably the link between 'Dan'el the righteous of Ezek. 14 and Ugarit A and 'Daniel the wise' of the Book of Daniel.

to distinguish between a simple folk-tale as told long ago and a cultivated revival which deliberately seeks to conform to the ancient pattern. The difficulty is to establish what in the Job story of the prologue and the epilogue is simple folk-tale (if any) and what is a sophisticated, cultivated pattern (if any).

We have in this Job story, prologue and epilogue, a simplicity which is combined with careful repetitions. We have the repetitions of numbers, the exact comparisons of what there was before the disasters and what there was after the restoration, the providential escape of one messenger from each disaster, the virtually similar way in which each messenger brings the bad tidings, the seven sons and the seven days, and a general repetition of phraseology. All these are evidence of the mechanics of the folk-tale, and the various legends which have come to light at Ugarit bear ample evidence of this custom of precise repetition: *Baal* I* 6.27, III 2.16, ? *Baal* (fragments) I B 16; also *Baal* V 3.31, V 4a.10, 24, 31; and these are examples from a considerable number. To what extent we have deliberate formalization and repetition in the Hebrew Job it is difficult to say. There is a formalism which belongs to the folk-tales of what are sometimes called 'primitive' peoples, though the better description is 'unsophisticated' or 'unconscious'. Note the repetitions which occur in the Brer Rabbit tales of Uncle Remus, and particularly compare the repetition of 'and I only am escaped to tell thee' with the repetition of 'en Brer Fox, he lay low', where in both cases the dramatic tension is heightened by the simple repetition of the phrase. Then for contrast, compare the conscientious and indeed the conscious simplicity of the modern revivalist folk-dance enthusiast with the unconscious enjoyment of the original folk-dancers—'earnest females' and 'self-conscious males' as against men and women simply enjoying themselves in simple fashion.

When the story opens, Job has seven sons and three daughters (1.2), and when the story ends he has seven (unless it is twice-seven, see above, pp. 4f.) sons and three daughters (42.13). Perhaps he never lost the daughters, but the facts are mentioned in a repetitive stylized manner. Each day there was a feast at one son's house, and there were seven sons, so that Job was able to round off each (sacred) seven-day period neatly with a sacrifice. It is curious that these three daughters should be given 'inheritance among their brethren' (42.15), since this is not at all in

accordance with Hebrew-Jewish law and custom.[17] No satisfactory solution of the problem of the anomaly of Job's property-
owning daughters has been proposed. Possibly Duhm was right
in suggesting that we have a remnant of a fuller story involving
the daughters of Job. A probable explanation is that the author
wants to say not only that they were beautiful, but that they were
wealthy also, and therefore wholly desirable in all the land on
both counts. We have suggested above[18] that perhaps it was
compensation for there being three and not six, whereas apparently some manuscripts at least thought that there were twice-
seven sons in the sequel of the story. At any rate LXX says that
there were none 'better' ($\beta\epsilon\lambda\tau\acute{\iota}o\upsilon\varsigma$? wealthier) 'under heaven',
since Job gave them property equally with their brothers. But
whatever the reason, there is something strange about the
daughters sharing the property with their brothers, and it may be
evidence of a man half-remembering an ancient custom and
getting it not quite right. Compare the difficulties of the *gō'ēl*-
story in the Book of Ruth: why should Boaz' having a son by
Ruth damage his own inheritance, and why the difference in the
rite of throwing the shoe? Both stories, that of Job and that of
Ruth, are 'modern' stories put into an ancient setting, with not
all details exactly right.

Job's property at the beginning of the story consisted of 'seven
thousand sheep and goats, and three thousand camels, and five
hundred yoke of oxen, and five hundred she-asses' (1.3). At the
end of the story the numbers are exactly doubled and all the numbers are carefully given; fourteen thousand, six thousand, one
thousand, one thousand. The seven sons, as we have seen, fit
exactly the seven 'sacred' days, and thus they can feast the whole
year round, one day at each house in turn (1.4), and every son as
host on his own regular day. Then at the end of each seven-day
cycle (1.5; the root is *nqp*, the same root as in Isa. 29.1, of the re-
curring cycle of the feasts), Job sent and hallowed (shrived) them.
He rose early in the dawn of this sacred taboo-day[19] to offer
whole-offerings, one for each son, in case any one of them had

---

[17] The analogy of the daughters of Zelophehad (Num. 27.1-11) is no
analogy at all, since, apart from other considerations, Zelophehad had no
sons. See further, N. H. Snaith, 'The Daughters of Zelophehad', *VT* 16
(1966) pp. 124-7.

[18] See above, p. 4.

[19] Cf. N. H. Snaith, *Jewish New Year Festival*, 1947, pp. 110-16.

committed any sin, broken any taboo or secretly nurtured any
untoward thought against God. We are here in the world of the
patriarchs, where the head of the family acts as sacrificing agent
and makes a straightforward, uncomplicated whole-offering as a
gift to God (Gen. 8.20; 22.2, 7, 13).

Various attempts have been made to fit these rites of Job (1.5)
into the Levitical scheme of the Priestly tradition. The first
attempt was as early as the LXX, where a whole line is introduced:
'and an ox for a sin-offering for them'. This is correct according
to Lev. 5.13-21, on the assumption that the seven brothers and
Job and the daughters are 'the whole assembly'. Alternatively,
an ox for a sin-offering is the biggest possible sin-offering. Perhaps the reason is that Job is being more than scrupulous in his
religious duties. Also, the first corrector of Codex Sin (possibly
the scribe himself) wrote καθαρισμόν (cleansing) for ἀριθμόν
(number), indeed a brilliant emendation. It shows how clever a
copyist could be in adapting what he found to what he believed
to be correct. It is incidentally a warning to us all that a brilliant
and clever emendation is not on that account sound. Other suggestions have been made: that Job summoned the sons to his
house, that he sent a priest to shrive them at their own homes,
that the root *qdš* (hallow) and the root *qr'* (bid, summon) are here
synonymous and both involve summoning to a sacred feast.[20] It
is best to leave the verse as it is, as indefinite, or rather as 'un-
developed ritualistically', as doubtless the author wrote it. Most
of all it is not wise to attempt to fit the details into the developed
sacrificial and hierarchical system of the Priestly tradition as out-
lined in Lev. 1-8, the ritual of the Second Temple. All that need be
said is that the intention of Job's whole-offering is close to that
of the compensation-offering.[21] This is the case where a man does
not know whether or not he has acted in such a manner as to involve someone else in loss,[22] so he brings his compensation-
offering in order to be perfectly sure that he has fulfilled all

[20] Driver-Gray, *Job*, ICC, p. 8, following T.

[21] *'āšām*, EVV 'guilt offering' of Lev. 5.17-19; cf. N. H. Snaith, *Leviticus
and Numbers*, Century Bible (new series), 1967, p. 51.

[22] See N. H. Snaith, 'The Sin-offering and the Guilt-offering', *VT* 15
(1965), pp. 73-80. The sin-offering is concerned with involuntary faults in
the breaking of taboos in the matter of sacred gifts and suchlike or in connection with things that are ritually unclean. The guilt-offering is concerned
with cases, both wilful and involuntary, in which damage has been done.

righteousness and that henceforth all will be well. This developed later into the *'āšām tālūy* (suspended guilt-offering) of the last years of the Second Temple.[23] This offering was brought every morning by the very, very scrupulous, those who were ultra-careful to fulfil every smallest detail of the Law. This is why the offering was also called the *'āšām-hah͏ᵃsīdīm* (the guilt-offering of the pious).[24] But Job's were not compensation-offerings (guilt-offerings), neither were they sin-offerings. They were whole-offerings, gifts to God, doubtless designed to be well-pleasing to him, but not influenced by that growing complication of ritual which seems to be inevitable in every religion and ultimately in every variant of every religion, even in those variants which begin by being anti-ritualistic. There is, however, a partial resemblance to the most expensive of all later sin-offerings, and this we take to be a sign that the author was a late writer seeking to give an archaic setting to his story.

The next scene in the story is the gathering of the heavenly court (1.6-8). This gathering takes place twice, and the phraseology is virtually the same in each case, with only the minimum variation demanded by the fact that the Satan is presenting himself for the second time. This type of repetition, as we saw in the Brer Rabbit stories and in the Ugarit tablets, is characteristic of folklore tales. Indeed, the differences in other passages in chs. 1 and 2 serve mainly to emphasize the repetitious elements involved. Compare 1.6 and 2.1: the wording is the same except for the addition in 2.1 of 'to present himself before the Lord'. See also 1.11 and 2.5: in 1.11 the Satan says, 'but put forth thine hand now, and touch *all that he hath*. I swear he will renounce thee to thy face', and in 2.5 he says, 'put forth thine hand now and touch *his bone and his flesh*. I swear he will renounce thee to thy face.'[25] Another repetition is in the introductory *wayᵉhī hayyōm*, lit. 'and the day came to be'. This phrase occurs three times without variation; 1.6; 1.13; 2.1.[26] Another formalized opening is to be

[23] See Ker III 1.

[24] Ker VI 3. *ḥāsīd*. This word came to be the technical word for the Jew who was wholly pious and loyal in fulfilling every detail of the Law; see N. H. Snaith, *The Distinctive Ideas of the Old Testament*, 1944, pp. 126f.

[25] In 1.12 and 2.6, 'in thy power' and 'in thy hand' (AV, RV) both stand for the same Hebrew word; RSV and JB correctly have 'in your power' in both cases, and DV the more literal 'in thy hand'.

[26] AV, RV, DV and JB have a different rendering in each case, and in 2.1 RSV differs from 1.6 and 1.13.

found in the introductions of the announcements of the various catastrophes which befell Job. In 1.16 we find, 'while he was yet speaking, there came another and said'. This is repeated in 1.17 and 1.18. Further, the tale of each messenger finishes with 'and I only am escaped to tell thee' (1.16; 1.17; 1.19). Again, 'and (they) have slain thy servants with the edge of the sword' is found in 1.15 and 1.17. The second gathering of the heavenly court and Job's subsequent troubles do not lend themselves to repetition in the same precise way, but the conclusion is partly the same: 'in all this Job did not sin' (1.22 and 2.10).

Another indication of the folk-lore element in the prologue is the testing of Job's righteousness. A parallel in Hindu legend is given by A. and M. Hanson.[27] There was a righteous king whose name was Harischandra. A supernatural being, a *rishi*, made a wager with another *rishi* that Harischandra was truly righteous and could not be tempted to do evil. The king survives every kind of distress and humiliation, but remains true. He performs his *dharma*. The ending is that the king's fortunes are restored. The righteous *rishi* wins and the wicked *rishi* loses. As the authors point out, the tale is concerned with Hindu righteousness, but the parallel is close. We judge that this kind of tale is part of the general store of folk-lore, and can be found in many areas, worked out according to the varying ideas of righteousness.[28]

We return to the statement concerning the length of Job's life after his restoration to prosperity (42.16). The Hebrew says that 'Job lived after this for a hundred and forty years', twice the allotted span of Ps. 90.10. The LXX '240 years in all' looks like an original 70 plus a second 70 with 100 added: there is considerable expansion in the last chapter of Job in LXX. The '140 years after this' of the Vulgate is double-70, presumably inspired by the statement of 42.10: 'twice as much as he had before'. What really matters from our present point of view is that the figures have the precise and formal nature which we find elsewhere in

---

[27] *The Book of Job*, p. 9.
[28] Compare the story of the massacre of the innocents in early Christian story, in the Moses legends and in the Math legends of the *Mabinogion*. See also the so-called Babylonian Job (below, pp. 21-27). Thus the general theme of the persecuted king (sheik) comes from the world's store of folk-lore. A more detailed examination of the Babylonian story supports a theory of definite knowledge of it on the part of the author of the Book of Job (below, pp. 26f.).

the story. Everything is worked out so carefully and so precisely that we seem to be dealing with a stylized folk-tale, an ancient tale retold in an archaic form for a more sophisticated age.

In this original Book of Job[29] we have a perfectly straight-forward and carefully-told tale. Job is the prosperous desert sheik. He and his family live in lordly luxury, aristocrats of the desert. Job himself is most scrupulous to avoid even the slightest error of any kind on his own part, and he goes to all lengths to put right any involuntary infringement by any member of his family group. God boasts before the heavenly court of Job's up-rightness and disinterested piety. In spite of a double dose of disaster—loss of all his property and dependants; grievous bodily pain, disgrace and discomfort—Job still holds fast. The Satan is defeated, having failed to prove that Job is no better than the rest of mankind. We hear no more of the Satan (why should we?). Job recants and is restored to favour and fortune, exactly twice as much as before. All his friends and relations come and console him for his previous sorrows, and all ends happily.

Very many scholars think that the author took the prologue and the epilogue from an early source, and all assume that the three friends were in his story from the beginning.[30]

But there are differences of opinion concerning the prologue and the epilogue. It is the mention of the three friends in the first three verses of the epilogue and what is said about them there that causes most of the trouble, and gives rise to the varied con-clusions of the scholars.[31] Certainly there is considerable agree-ment that in one way or another prologue plus epilogue on the one side and dialogue on the other side do not properly belong to each other. We are of the opinion that Dhorme and Hölscher were right when they say that the author wrote both prologue and epilogue himself as a folk-lore story.

The patience of Job has become proverbial. This is the Job of

[29] Shortened prologue and epilogue; chs. 3; 29-31; Yahweh's speeches, Job's repentance.

[30] See the long list in H. H. Rowley, 'The Book of Job and its Meaning', *Bulletin of the John Rylands Library* 41 (1958), p. 177. The list includes Well-hausen, Budde, Cheyne, Duhm, Volz, Oesterley and Robinson, etc. etc. Add particularly Fohrer; also S. Terrien, 'Introduction and Exegesis of Job', *IB*, III, 1954, pp. 887-1198.

[31] Koenig and R. Simon reject the prologue; Buttenweiser and Finkelstein reject the epilogue. Stevenson thinks that both prologue and epilogue are taken from an earlier prose work and were later joined to the dialogue.

our first edition of the book. The Job of the dialogue is not patient, far from it. He is argumentative, often on the edge of exasperation and sometimes most violent in his speech.

II

THE ORIGIN OF THE STORY OF JOB

It is generally agreed that wisdom was by way of being international during the millennium before Christ—perhaps in the previous millennium also—and that it was far from being confined to Israel alone. By 'international' we mean the known world of the time, as it would be known by the inhabitant of Palestine who raised his eyes beyond the borders of his own country: Egypt, through Edom, Palestine, Syria and on to Babylonia. This literature is characterized by speculations concerning human life, what it is and perhaps what it ought to be, how to live it, the why and the wherefore of it, why men suffer and what, if anything, the gods have to do with it.[1]

The particular question often asked is: Is there any source outside Israel, not so much for wisdom literature in general, as for the Book of Job in particular? There are seven ancient texts to be taken into consideration: three Egyptian, three Babylonian and one Sumerian.

The first of the Egyptian texts is 'The Complaints of the Eloquent Peasant', as it has been called.[2] This consists of a prologue and an epilogue in prose, and, contained within these, nine speeches of a more poetic type. If the three cycles of speeches in the Book of Job had been complete, we would have had nine speeches there also. Perhaps there was a nine-speech model which the author of the Book of Job was seeking to copy. The Egyptian work in its present shape belongs to the twentieth to eighteenth centuries BC. The second of the Egyptian texts is 'The Prophecy of Nefer-Rohu', as it has been called,[3] where once again we have a poetic piece within two prose pieces. The third Egyptian text is 'A Dispute over Suicide'.[4] The papyrus is from the Middle

---

[1] For evidence as to the cosmopolitan nature of these speculations, see M. Noth and D. Winton Thomas, eds., *Wisdom in Israel and in the Ancient East, Presented to Professor Harold Henry Rowley*, VTS, III, (1955).

[2] J. A. Wilson, *ANET*, pp. 407-10.

[3] J. A. Wilson, *ANET*, pp. 444-6.

[4] J. A. Wilson, *ANET*, pp. 405-7; T. W. Thacker, *DOTT*, pp. 162-7.

Kingdom, as is the first of these three Egyptian texts, but in this case we certainly have a copy of an older work, which may well date from 2280-2000 BC. The beginning has been lost, but we have first a short piece of prose in which the writer's soul answers what the writer apparently has already said, and this is followed by the writer's answer to his soul, all of which is in verse. The conclusion is the soul's advice, and this is short and again in prose. The text deals with a man who has been grievously maltreated, but his complaints deal rather with the decadence of human society in general. He wishes to die and proposes to have done with life, but in the prose conclusion his soul bids him cast care aside, and hold on till both soul and body find rest at last in the West.

The first of the Babylonian texts has been variously called 'The Babylonian Theodicy', 'The Babylonian Ecclesiastes', 'A Dialogue about Human Misery'.[5] The date is probably between 1400 and 1000 BC. Two-thirds of it survive and it originally consisted of an acrostic of twenty-seven stanzas, eleven lines to a stanza. The eleven lines of each stanza open with the same sign, and the signs of the twenty-seven stanzas form an acrostic which reads: 'I, Saggil-kinam-ubbib, the incantation-priest, am benediction-priest of the god and the king.' The problem is that of the righteous man who suffers, combined with questions as to where justice is to be found and what, if anything, the gods have to do with it. The poem takes the form of a dialogue in which the sufferer and his friend alternate throughout, stanza by stanza. The second of the Babylonian texts has been called 'A Pessimistic Dialogue between Master and Servant'.[6] All the activities of human life are discussed, to be praised and then shown to be futile. This applies to power and ambition, all kinds of pleasures, including women, business, forgiveness and religion. The dialogue is formal rather than real; the slave agreed with everything the master says. It is as though the author regarded himself as necessarily involved in a dialogue form, and satisfied convention by introducing the slave who says very little more than 'yes'. The third of the Babylonian texts is the so-called 'Babylonian Job'.[7]

The Sumerian text has been called 'Man and his God'.[8] The

[5] W. G. Lambert, *DOTT*, pp. 97-103; R. H. Pfeiffer, *ANET*, pp. 438-40.
[6] R. H. Pfeiffer, *ANET*, pp. 437-8.　　　　　　[7] See below, pp. 21-27.
[8] S. N. Kramer, *Wisdom in Israel and in the Ancient Near East*, ed. M. Noth, et al., VTS, III (1955), pp. 170-82.

date is c. 1700 BC, but the original may well be 300 years earlier. Like the Babylonian Job, the poem opens with praise to the god. It proceeds to deal with a wealthy, wise and righteous man who is suddenly overwhelmed by sickness and pain. With tears and earnest prayer he turns to his god, who is moved with compassion for him, saves him from his troubles and restores him to prosperity and joy. There is no dialogue.

In these Near Eastern texts and in the Hebrew Book of Job there are various common features. We have a framework of two sections of prose with verse in between. We have dialogues, and in one instance it would appear that the author thought a dialogue was essential at all costs. The general theme is the inequality of human fate, the apparent injustice in the suffering of the righteous, all combined with the problem of the relation between God and man. The Book of Job, therefore, is part of a general corpus of wisdom literature belonging to the Near East and covering the whole of the fertile crescent. It is much later, at least a thousand years later, than extant writings of the same type in other areas of the Near East. This agrees with what we know concerning other matters: prosperity and the consequent leisure which gives men time to think are a much later development among the Hebrews than similar movements in the urban areas of Egypt and Mesopotamia. There is no direct dependence on the part of the Book of Job on any of these six texts which we have described, but there is a general similarity of style and format, and the content of thought is from the same basic origin.

We turn to the third of the Babylonian texts, the so-called 'Babylonian Job' ('I Will Praise the Lord of Wisdom'). We find here a remarkable similarity with what we have called the first draft of the Hebrew Book of Job, a similarity so remarkable that it can scarcely be accidental. This means that while the author of the Book of Job was influenced by the wisdom literature of the Near East in general, he was influenced by the Babylonian Job in particular.

The so-called 'Babylonian Job' is ancient, certainly older than the time of Hammurabi (c. 1728-1686 BC), but known from copies and commentaries of the seventh century BC and from a fragment found at Sippar.[9] The seventh-century tablets are copies of

---

[9] For translations of the text of the 'Babylonian Job', see R. W. Rogers, *Cuneiform Parallels to the Old Testament*, 1912, pp. 164-9 and a selection from

ancient Babylonian texts, copied by Asshur-bani-pal's scribes. They were found in his library among the ruins of Nineveh. Originally there were four tablets. Of the first only a few lines survive, rather more of the third and fourth, but most of the second. This means that we must beware of reading into the gaps what is favourable to our own point of view, as the ritual-pattern advocates have tended to do in their descriptions of the New Year Festival at Babylon.[10]

According to a commentary published by Rawlinson,[11] of which there is a German translation in M. Jastrow,[12] the name of the sufferer is Tabi-utul-Bel, a king who lived in Nippur, and this statement is generally accepted. Morris Jastrow[13] thinks it possible that the Babylonian tale is the prototype of the Hebrew Job story, though there is no evidence of any direct connection between the two. There is indeed little, if any, literary connection, but there are traditions which associate Job with the Hauran and even with the Euphrates. According to Chrysostom and Isho-dad, Job's home was actually in Edom. Against this there is a strong tradition, up to the fourth century in Christian circles and strong also in Muslim tradition, which connects Job with the Hauran. This may be due to an interpretation of 'the sons of the East' (Job 1.3) in the light of Gen. 29.1, Judg. 6.3, etc. The link with Edom is developed in the LXX, according to which Jobab-Job succeeded Balak as a king in Edom (Job 17.17d), though Codex A has a reference to 'the boundaries of the Euphrates'. Incidentally, in the LXX the three friends are said to be three kings; cf. the Western Christian tradition which has made the Magi become not only three (so the Western tradition) but also Kings of Orient.

---

this translation in S. R. Driver and G. B. Gray, *A Critical and Exegetical Commentary on the Book of Job*, ICC, 1921, pp. xxxi-xxxiii. A more elegant, though less literal translation is to be found in M. Jastrow, Jr., 'The Babylonian Job', CR, xv (December, 1908), pp. 801-8. See also M. Jastrow, *Die Religion Babyloniens und Assyriens*, 1912, II. i, pp. 121-31, and R. H. Pfeiffer, *ANET*, pp. 434-7.

[10] See S. G. F. Brandon, 'The Myth and Ritual Position Critically Considered', *Myth, Ritual and Kingship*, ed. S. H. Hooke, 1958, p. 270: he argues that the documents are relatively late; and the ritual for the sixth to the eleventh day is lost—this includes the time when the sacred marriage 'must' have taken place.

[11] *Cuneiform Inscriptions of Western Asia*, V, Pl. 47, rev. 5.

[12] *Die Religion* II. i, pp. 130f.

[13] *CR*, xv, p. 801.

Driver and Gray[14] find no Babylonian association whatever. They say that there is nothing in the Babylonian Job to compare with the combination of narrative and discourse such as is found in the Hebrew Job. This certainly is true, but the fact that so little of the first tablet is available makes it difficult to be sure what was and what was not in the original Babylonian work. In any case, their objections do not apply to our proposal, which involves originally no dialogue at all. They say also that there is a sharp and crucial difference between the two works on the matter of guilt. 'Yahweh in the prologue and Job in his speeches agree in asserting the innocence of Job's character.' This certainly is the case, and it is particularly true of chs. 3; 29-31 which we have called Job's soliloquy. But Driver and Gray go on to say: 'On the other hand, the Babylonian sufferer, though he is conscious of having been punctilious in the discharge of duties the neglect of which would have explained his sufferings, is anything but certain that he has not committed some sin which, unknown to him, may have been displeasing to the gods and therefore the cause of his sufferings.' This, in our view, is an overstatement. All we can find to suggest that the Babylonian sufferer allows that perhaps he may unwittingly have committed some sin, is in the second tablet, lines 33-37, which in Jastrow's translation[15] are:

> What, however, seems good to me may be displeasing to a god:
> What to one's mind may seem bad, may find favour with a god;
> Who is there that can grasp the will of the gods in heaven?
> The plan of a god, full of mystery, who can understand it?
> How can mortals fathom the way of a god?

This means, at most, that no man can understand a god, and that so far as the gods are concerned the whole matter of right and wrong is a complete mystery. It is not that 'he more or less clearly admits he has done amiss'. We do not find this. He may have admitted it, or he may not have admitted it, but the same applies to everybody. The author of the Babylonian Job then goes on to discuss those sudden changes in human life whereby a man may be fit and well one night and dead by morning. The whole context is concerned with the sudden and inexplicable changes of fortune among men in general, and not particularly with any sin which Tabi-utul-bel may have committed.

---

[14] *Job*, p. xxxiv.   [15] *CR*, xv, p. 805.

There are some other lines which may have influenced Driver and Gray. These are on the same tablet and on the same side of it (lines 4-9). Jastrow translates them as follows:

> I cried to the god, but he did not show his countenance:
> I invoked the goddess, but she did not raise her head.
> The omen priest could not determine the outcome:
> The diviner could not clear up my case through the offering.
> To the oracle priest I appealed, but he told me nothing:
> The exorciser could not by his rites release me from the ban.

These lines say that the sufferer tried every means to get free from his troubles, but that no cult official could assure him of better times to come. There is nothing about any possible sin. Or again, Driver and Gray point out the differences in name and country between the two writings. There certainly are differences, but there is nothing in what we have of the Babylonian poem itself to indicate any name or country. Whatever identifications of this type there are, are to be found in the commentary. Similarly, there is nothing in the poetic portions of the biblical Job to indicate name or origin, neither in what Job says, nor, for that matter, in what the friends say. It is in the prologue and the epilogue that we find these details. In this respect the two poems are similar: the geographical details are in the commentary and in the prose section and the rubrics.

It is plain that there is no direct connection between the Babylonian Job and the Hebrew Job. The matter and the mode of expression of the former are entirely Mesopotamian; the matter and the mode of expression of the latter are Hebraic, though of a specialized nature. It is wisdom poetry, and the vocabulary is peculiarly different from elsewhere in the Old Testament. Many more rare words are used which can be explained from other Semitic languages, and many words are used with earlier meaning which have survived. Indeed in these respects the only book which approaches Job to the extent to which all this is the case is Proverbs, the other large scale wisdom book in the Old Testament. Nevertheless we maintain that, the general theme of the Babylonian Job and the general theme of Job 3; 29-31 and 38-39 is the same.

On the first tablet, of which only a small portion survives, we find:

> A king—I have been transformed into a slave;
> My companions avoided me as a madman;
> I was cast aside by my own circles.

With this compare Job 31.1-15. The phraseology is different and the setting is different, but the turning against the speaker by those who formerly had honoured him and treated him with respect is found in both poems. In each case the speaker was originally the highest in the land; in the one he was a king, in the other he was leading citizen and chief judge.

On the second tablet, lines 4-5, we read:

> I cried to the god, and he did not show his face:
> I prayed to the goddess, but she did not lift her head.

As we have seen above, the writer goes on to say that he has sought the services of every kind of priest, and wizard, This, of course, has no parallel in the Hebrew poem, but compare Job 30. 20:

> I cry to thee, but thou dost not answer:
> I stand in prayer, but thou takest no notice of me.

Again, on the second tablet, lines 12-22, we have the sufferer's claim that he has always taken pains to do what is right, and now he is suffering as though he had actually done all the wrong things. But the curious thing is that his good deeds are recounted in a strangely negative way. He says:

> As though I had not always set aside a portion for the god;
> As though I had not always remembered the goddess with food;
> As though I had not always bowed my face and shown my humility;
> As though I had passed over the festal day of the god;

and so on, 'observed the moon festival', etc., etc.

With this compare Job 31.15-34, where we get the same kind of negative statement, though this time the matter is ethical rather than ritualistic, as one would expect in wisdom literature.[16]

---

[16] But with Job 31.15-34 compare also the second of the nine tablets which compose the *Shurpu* (burning series): Zimmern, 'Die Beschwörungstafeln Shurpu', *Beitrage zur Kenntniss der Babylonischen Religion*, 1901, pp. 1ff. and R. W. Rogers, *Religion of Babylonia and Assyria*, 1908, pp. 157ff. It is described as 'an incantation with ethical contents', and in it there are over sixty lines which contain a detailed list of possible sins, expressed in the same partly negative, partly positive way.

We sum up the details of our comparison of the Babylonian Job and the Hebrew Job:

Job 3 tells of the longing of Job that he had never been born, and of his hope for the oblivion of the world of the dead where everything is forgotten and all are at peace. Chapter 29 tells of his former glories, but ch. 30 gives the contrast and tells of his fall from splendour and honour. Much of the first tablet of the Babylonian Job is missing, but in the part which has survived and can be read we have the tragedy of his present circumstances: he is cast aside by his former associates, treated as a slave and a madman. It is naturally tempting to suggest that the missing part of the first tablet contained a statement of the king's former glory and that what we have is the tail-end of the contrast between the former affluence and honour and the present poverty and disgrace. Then there is in the second tablet a detailed account of what the sufferer has not done and not omitted to do, and all of this comparable to Job 31.15-34. There is also a detailed description of the victim's sufferings; Jastrow, *CR*, xv, p. 805 and Job 30. 16-31.

We agree that there is no case for assuming any connection between the Babylonian Job and the Hebrew Job as a whole. The objections of Driver and Gray are valid to this extent. But the comparison which we have made is between the Babylonian Job and what we have called the first edition of the Hebrew Job; i.e. the shorter prologue, the shorter epilogue, and chs. 3; 29-31 plus the Yahweh speeches in 38-39; 40.6-41.26. The parallels in motif and style between the Babylonian Job and Job 3; 29-31 are in our view remarkable: the contrast between then and now; the turning away of former friends (the three friends were not in the story at this stage, and the relations did not turn up until all was well again); the detailed description of the sufferings; the curiously negative account of his right actions; the restoration by the god (fourth tablet). We do not know whether in the first and fourth tablets of the Babylonian Job there was any speech by the god; too little of these tablets is extant. But the king becomes a slave, and the desert sheik sits outcast on the dunghill. The king has done everything he can think of to please the god and the goddess; Job has been scrupulous beyond words, in the prologue with the proper sacrifices and in the poem with the most careful ethical conduct. But the matter is all different. The Babylonian Job is essentially Babylonian, with his favourite god and goddess and the exorcisers and magicians and the like; the Hebrew Job is Hebrew with the ancient nomadic setting, the strictly monotheistic background, the absence of wizards and priests and suchlike. The Babylonian Job is Babylonian wisdom literature; the Hebrew Job is Hebrew wisdom literature. But the same problem is described and discussed in the same way. The Babylonian enquiry into conduct is concerned with the ritual of Babylonian religion; the Hebrew enquiry is concerned with those ideas of conduct which are set out in the Deuteronomic laws as to how to treat one's neighbour, and especially the underprivileged.

Our conclusion, therefore, is that when the Hebrew author wrote his first draft of the Book of Job, he found his technical inspiration, his method and his basic theme in the Babylonian Job. The general outline of the Hebrew Job (first draft) is that of the Babylonian Job, and the method of dealing with the problem is the same. But the content of the Hebrew Job is truly and essentially Hebrew. There is plenty of evidence for the interchange in ancient times of wisdom ideas and even of wisdom literature.[17] The Hebrew writer was a first-class author. He reconstructed the ancient, simple prose as he retold the folk-tale, and he composed any number of superb and elegant synonymous couplets in the verse part of his book. But he owed his primary literary inspiration directly to the Babylonian Job.

We turn to another characteristic of wisdom literature common to both inside and outside Israel. This is the strong emphasis there is upon sickness and illness of every kind.

The first references to sickness appear in the prologue, in 2.7f., where it is said that Job was afflicted with painful boils from head to foot. Apparently these boils involved an intolerable itching.[18] Many attempts have been made at a diagnosis, the most recent being 'a very extensive erythema', an extensive surface inflammation of the skin. There is nothing in the Hebrew which demands an open, running sore, though this is not necessarily ex-

[17] See Prov. 22.17-23.14, which is taken virtually as a whole from the Egyptian *The Teaching of Amen-em-ope*. See further A. Causse, 'Sagesse égyptienne et sagesse juive', *Revue d'Histoire et de Philosophie Religieuses*, 9 (1929), pp. 149-69, and H. Ranston, *The Old Testament Wisdom Books and their Teaching*, 1930.

[18] The Hebrew *šᵉḥîn* means 'inflammation', cf. Arabic *saḫuna* (to be hot, inflamed), Syriac *šᵉḥen*, Ugarit *šḥn* (*H* 2.38, was feverish).

cluded. The description in Job 2.7f. corresponds exactly with that
of the sickness of Deut. 28.35, *šᵉḥīn rāʿ* (a bad boil), but from head
to foot. This is the infection which is known as 'the boil of Egypt'
in Deut. 25.27. Hezekiah's illness involved a *šᵉḥīn*, and this was
treated with a fig plaister; II Kings 20.7 and Isa. 38.21. Such a
boil might be 'leprosy', Lev. 13.18, 19, 20: Hebrew *ṣāraʿat*. It
would depend on whether or not it was an open sore. In Lev. 13
the test is either a depression in the skin or an ulceration. Sores and
blebs and such like come under suspicion because they may spread
and become open sores. The man whose skin becomes white all
over is not a 'leper', but if an open sore appears then he is a leper.
If this open sore heals, then he ceases to be a leper even though
his skin is white all over (Lev. 13.13). Most of the ritually unclean
rules in Leviticus are connected with raw wounds or the discharge of pus or blood or semen. The contagion is ritual, not
clinical. There may be clinical contagion, but this is not the point
with which the priests were primarily concerned. They were concerned with ritual uncleanness and ritual contagion. We conclude
that the Job of the prologue was afflicted with the traditional 'boil
of Egypt' (Ex. 9.9-11), though apparently LXX considered it to
be 'leprosy'. The MT says that Job 'sat among the ashes' (2.8), a
sign of disgrace and penitence, but LXX makes him sit 'on the
dunghill outside the city'. This makes him a leper, especially since,
according to LXX, the potsherd of v. 8 is 'to scrape away the
discharge', which the MT does not say. This 'boil of Egypt' is the
traditional dreadful and disgraceful disease of the wicked, and it is
because it is the ultimate disgrace and the recognized ultimate
proof of the divine displeasure that the Satan inflicts this upon
Job. Many diseases have been suggested, but they have been based
partly on the assumption that the prologue and the soliloquy and
the speeches are to be considered together.[19]

There are various symptoms described in the soliloquy. In
3.24 Job cannot eat for sighing, he groans continually, he is overcome by terror and fear, and he cannot find any ease or relief.
In 30.17 he says that by night all his bones are pierced with pain,
and his fleshless bones will not lie still (though the reference may

---

[19] See Driver and Gray, *Job*, pp. 22-24 and the references given there. To
these add the suggestion of S. Terrien (*IB*, III, p. 920), *pemphigus foliaceus*, but,
as Terrien says, 'no diagnosis can be assured'. This is because in the poetic
parts of the book, it is no disease in particular, but all diseases in general.

be to raw nerves).[20] Verse 18 is so difficult that some scholars give it up altogether. Apparently Job's clothes are wholly disfigured and stiff with discharges from his body (or mouth), and with dried matter and pus, so that they cause him extreme discomfort because of the constrictions they impose upon him. In 30.27 he says that his bowels are in continual ferment, and he sees no prospect of betterment in the future: 'days of affliction are waiting for me'. If this is a factual description, it looks like an acute case of dysentery, perhaps amoebic dysentery with all its added prostration. But in 30.30 he says that his skin goes black and peels off, and that fever is burning up his bones. The impression to be gathered from all these symptoms is that the sufferer is describing more than one disease.

This is confirmed by statements in the dialogue, the other parts of the book, that is the chapters between the end of ch. 3 and the beginning of ch. 29. In 6.7 (Job's reply to Eliphaz in the first cycle), Job says that his stomach revolts at the thought of food. The second half of this verse is difficult. LXX took it to mean that he found the smell of his food as offensive as the smell of a lion, but it probably means as offensive as vomited food.[21] In 7.3-6 we have a picture of great and continuous misery. When he lies down,[22] he longs to get up. When he gets up, he wishes it were night-time again. He tosses about all night, and wanders about all day. His body is covered with maggots and filth; his skin keeps on scabbing and breaking out again. He feels that his time is running out, and that his days flash past as quickly as the heddle of a loom. In 7.14 he speaks of being terrified by bad dreams and nightmares. It is worse than being strangled, and he wishes he were dead. He does not get even a moment's respite. In 19.17 he speaks of his breath being loathsome to his wife, and of himself as being loathsome to his own kinsfolk. He is reduced to skin and bone (19.20), and LXX thinks of his flesh being rotten underneath his skin.

The Book of Job is by no means unique in this multiplication of symptoms. The same kind of thing is found elsewhere,

---

[20] Cf. Arabic *'araqat* (nerve). Nachmanides said the Hebrew word means 'veins', Arabic *'irq*.

[21] Read *zihámāh kidᵉwi* (is foul as in illness).

[22] Translate: 'When I lie down, I say "When will it be day?" When I arise, again, "When will it be evening?" And I am full of restless wandering until twilight.' This, in part, follows LXX.

especially in the penitential Psalms, 6; 32; 38; 51; 102; 130; 143.[23]
In Ps. 6.2 (MT 3) the psalmist is utterly wearied and exhausted.
He says: 'My bones are withered and dying.'[24] He is full of tears
and sorrow the whole night long, so that his bed is wet with tears
(v. 6, MT 7). His eye is wasting away with grief. In Ps. 32.3
(MT 4) the psalmist says that his bones (i.e. the moisture of the
living bone as against the dry porosity of the long-dead bone: cf.
Ezek. 37.1-10) are changed into a dryness comparable only to the
drought of late summer, when the blazing sun beats down from a
cloudless sky on an earth already dusty and parched. Ps. 38 provides us with a tremendous catalogue of woes: no soundness in
his flesh, bent and bowed down, his loins filled with burning,
faint and sore and bruised, palpitations (10, MT 11), failing
strength, blind, everybody keeps away from him, as if deaf and
dumb—altogether, everything short of death and absolute dis-
solution seems to have descended upon the poor man. Ps. 51 has
not the same detailed description of ailments and physical
afflictions, but apparently the suppliant's bones are broken
(v. 8, MT 10). In Ps. 102 we have more distressing details: fever
in his bones (v. 3, MT 4), heart smitten and withered like grass,
forgets to eat his food, his bones stick through his skin, withered
like grass in high summer. Ps. 130 is free from allusions to sickness
and Ps. 143 speaks only of desolation. But the general picture of
these seven psalms is of a man heaped over with and submerged
in all the physical distresses to which mortal man is heir. Other
psalms speak of considerable physical distress: 22.14-17 (MT
15-18); 31.9f. (MT 10f.); 55.4f. (MT 5f.); 88; but the descriptions
of dire sickness and distress are either connected with the per-
secution of the righteous poor, or, especially in the penitential
psalms, associated with sin.

In discussions of the Hebrew penitential psalms, references are
frequently made to the Babylonian penitential psalms, and indeed
there are many similarities. There is, for instance, the 'Prayer of
Lamentations to Ishtar',[25] which, apart from the names of
Babylonian gods and references to 'my lady', might easily be a
Hebrew penitential psalm and might even be taken from Job's
soliloquy. The suppliant's 'wretched body' is full of confusion and

[23] See N. H. Snaith, *The Seven Psalms*, 1964, pp. 23f.
[24] Read *nābᵉlū* (so Perles), the same root as *nᵉbēlā* (corpse).
[25] F. J. Stephens, *ANET*, pp. 383-5.

trouble: he refers to his sick heart, his wretched intestines, bitter mourning (lines 46-50). He suffers from 'sickness, headache, loss and destruction' (line 69). In another Babylonian penitential psalm, one to which there has been given the title 'Prayer to Every God',[26] the sufferer is in great pain and distress. Here once more we have the situation where the sufferer does not know which god or goddess he has offended, nor what transgressions he has committed, though, judging apparently from his grievous misfortunes he thinks they must be very great indeed. What he does know for certain is that some god or goddess has oppressed him and placed him under stress of great suffering. His transgressions must be 'seven times seven', and he prays again and again for their removal. The idea of suffering from an unknown sin seems to be a feature, almost an obsession, in all this wisdom literature in the whole area from Egypt through to Mesopotamia. The reason is plain: the accepted theory is that disease and misfortune are the inevitable results of sin. The sufferer is not aware of any sin which he has committed. Therefore he must have committed some sin of which he is not aware. All this is strangely parallel to Job and his problem, though here there is the marked difference (ch. 31) that Job insists upon his integrity whatever the 'popular', orthodox evidence may say against him. But generally in this wisdom literature, and to some extent also in Job, we find a searching for a possible sin. This same situation is found in the Hittite 'Prayer of Kantuzilis for Relief from his Sufferings'.[27] Here there is the searching for a sin, and a denial that the sufferer has committed any particular sin. There is a list of all the things he has not done: he has never broken an oath made in the god's name; he has never eaten holy food, he has never brought impurity on to his body; he has never starved any animal; he has never eaten food or drunk water indiscriminately— if only he could be told his fault. . . .

We have already discussed at length the Babylonian Job, but in that poem also we have descriptions of many ills and sicknesses: beaten with a whip, pierced with a shaft, limbs undone, covered with excrement on his bed, symptoms of fever (second tablet, reverse, lines 5-13).

Our conclusion is that in the Near East generally the recitation

---

[26] F. J. Stephens, *ANET*, pp. 391-2.
[27] A. Goetze, *ANET*, pp. 400f.

of serious symptoms of the most dreadful illnesses was the regular and conventional way of confessing sin and of seeking forgiveness (and healing) from the god. There are no specific illnesses described in any of these poems. This is why scholars have found it difficult to identify them and have varied so much in their diagnosis. They are all partly right, and all equally right. '*Everybody* has won, and *all* must have prizes', as the Dodo said. The prayers are penitential prayers and this is why they are cast in this particular mould. The more penitent a man is, the more ghastly are the symptoms which he describes. It is helped by the human failing whereby we all tend to exaggerate our symptoms when we describe them to someone else. (I have never heard any man say that he has had '(single) pneumonia'; it is always 'double pneumonia'.) When a man sins, he meets with trouble and sickness. (This is not true. Sometimes he does; sometimes he does not. But this was orthodox opinion.) And vice versa, when a man meets with troubles and sickness, it is because he has sinned. (This contains all the weakness of a converse fallacy: it is not necessarily true, in spite of the prayers for the sick in the Book of Common Prayer.) Some of these psalms are very, very penitent, and some labour under a tremendous conviction of sin. This is the way in which he expresses his penitence and his conviction of sin. It is not any kind of masochism or morbidity, though presumably it might easily develop into either or both, and at various periods in the history of Christendom it has done so. It is to be found here in Job and in the penitential psalms because of the close connection which all men believed to exist between sin and suffering. John 9.2: 'Rabbi, who did sin, this man, or his parents, that he should be born blind?' To which Jesus answered: 'Neither did this man sin, nor his parents . . .'

In conclusion: the author of the Book of Job has produced a typical Near East wisdom writing, and he has reproduced the traditional characteristics of similar writings from Mesopotamia, Egypt and the Hittite country. He has been inspired in particular by the poem known to us as 'The Babylonian Job', but in characteristic Hebrew fashion he has transformed it into his own religious world. The Hebrew Job differs from the rest because it is essentially and unreservedly monotheistic. It differs from the rest because its ethics are sound Deuteronomic ethics, even to the care of the underprivileged classes of Hebrew daily life. This

Hebrew writer is not concerned about ritual offences (not, that is, in the poetic sections), nor is he interested in ritual uncleanness and the taboos which depend upon this. These things belong to priestly orthodoxy. This man is concerned with sin, that rebellion which separates man from God. He is the wise man of Israel who has learned something from the prophets, but he finds himself involved in the traditional forms of wisdom writing and this is why he has adopted this method of a prose prologue and a prose epilogue, with a poetic section in between consisting of the sufferer's laments and the reply of God.[28]

[28] An example of how an author found himself in ancient times constricted by the formal shape of those books which were, so to speak, the tools of his trade is the evangelist Luke. Both in the Gospel and in Acts he opens with a dedication to one Theophilus. Lagarde sought to show that in his use of such a preface Luke was influenced by the *Materia Medica* of Dioscurides (a contemporary), and others have mentioned Galen and Hippocrates, all to show that both before and after Luke's time, this is the way in which medical treatises were written. Actually, such a preface was a common literary feature of the period. The author dedicated his work to his patron: Dioscurides to Areioss, Josephus (*Contra Apion*) to Epaphroditus. Luke may not have deliberately followed the pattern of medical treatises, but, having some pretensions to literary merit, he found himself constrained to follow the customary pattern of his day and literary craft.

III

THE FIRST BOOK OF JOB

We believe the original Hebrew Job, the first edition, to have
consisted of: The shorter prologue and the shorter epilogue (no
reference to the three friends), Job's soliloquy (3; 29-31), Yahweh's
speeches (38-39; 40.6-41.26), Job's apology (40.1-5) and Job's
humble submission (parts of 42.1-6).

1. Job's Soliloquy

(a) Chapter 3

This chapter bewails the lot of a man who has been born to
nothing but trouble. It is not a description of every man; the
speaker is talking about his own troubles. The verse which is
traditionally quoted as being descriptive of the inevitable sorrow
and burden of human life ('Man is born to trouble, as the sparks
fly upward') is not in a speech by Job, but is in Eliphaz's first
speech (5.7). In any case it should be translated: 'A man begets
his own trouble, as surely as the sparks fly high.'[1] This happens
when the wood-fire is interfered with, though perhaps it is not
legitimate to press the poet's simile so far. In ch. 3 we find the
complaint of a man whose own lot is unease, disquiet and continual trouble (v. 26). Job means himself, and he wishes he had
never been born, or if born, buried as soon as born. This is
followed by a picture of the world of the dead as a place of free-
dom from toil and trouble. This is not the usual picture of Sheol
with its dreariness and lifelessness, but of death as a happy release
from pain and toil, and from all the woes of an unequal world.
The chapter ends with Job turning back to meditate on his own
desperate state. There is no charge made against God, and no
problem is discussed.

(b) Chapter 29

In this chapter we have a picture of Job's earlier prosperity, but

---

[1] Read *yōlīd* (Böttcher); cf. JB. Note the previous verse which says that
affliction and trouble are not automatic.

it is not a portrayal of the life of the wealthy desert sheik of the prologue, whose property is in sheep and goats, camels, cattle and she-asses. The setting in v. 7, for instance, is of a settled agricultural community with walled settlements, a setting closely similar to that of Ruth 4.1. Both in Job 29 and in Ruth 4 we have a deliberately contrived archaic setting. Here in Job 29 the speaker walks down the street to take his place at the local council in the open space at the town gate ('*ir* is 'a walled city', but more 'walled' than 'city'). There in the open space he occupies his customary seat, theoretically among his equals, but in prestige *primus inter pares* and even *princeps inter pares*. This is the regular court-house of old Israel. Meanwhile all pay him the greatest respect. The youngsters hide their faces and the older men rise to their feet. The speaker is the perfect example of the grandee of that society. He is the man who has prospered, has risen to high estate and is universally respected. He is the perfect pattern of what the good man of Deuteronomy would be in a primitive society—at least, it is in such terms that the author describes him. He dispenses justice as a good Deuteronomist should: eyes to the blind, feet to the lame, the guardian and protector of all that are in need and have no helper.

(c) Chapter 30

In this chapter we have the contrast to ch. 29. No reversal of fortune could be more complete. The speaker is now jeered at by the rabble. Everything has gone wrong. He still can stand up in the assembly, but now it is only to ask for assistance. He is outcast in the desert, and all is sorrow and tears. As in chs. 3 and 29, no charge is made against God and the problem of Job's change of fortune is not discussed. We take 29.21-23 to be statements of fact rather than charges of injustice.

(d) Chapter 31

In this chapter Job repeatedly swears on oath that he is innocent and therefore ought not to have suffered. Orthodox opinion maintained that calamity and ruin are the fate of evil-doers. Job does not dispute that orthodox opinion is right, but he is nevertheless quite certain that all he has suffered has happened to a man who is innocent. Job is quite willing to stand trial and to suffer whatever punishment he may have deserved, and he is sure that if once his case is heard, all will be well. In this chapter, then, we have bewilderment, but not the argumentative attitude which Job adopts in the dialogue with the three friends. No charge is made against God, nor is orthodoxy questioned.

Many scholars think that there has been considerable displacement in this chapter. The first four verses are not in the true LXX text. Of these verses, 2-4 belong together, but 1b is a curious line to be where it is. When, later in the chapter, the speaker is saying that he has not done this or that particular wrong thing, he does not come to the matter of women until v. 9. Also, vv. 35-37 interrupt the catalogue of sinful actions which the speaker swears he has not committed, much as vv. 2-4 appear to be an interruption where they are. It is possible that, as Driver-Gray (*Job*) suggest, vv. 38-40 are misplaced and should come elsewhere, though there is much difference of opinion as to where they should be placed. Our guess is that vv. 38-40 should follow v. 34, so that vv. 35-37 come at the end of the chapter, but before the rubric.

But are vv. 2-4 an interruption? Our view is that the trouble is in v. 1 and not in vv. 2-4. Why should Job bind himself by oath only so far as his own eyes are concerned (if this is how *le'ēnāy* is to be translated)? Perhaps the key to the problem is in the very early variation in Codex Sin, the correction which Swete designates with an asterisk, a correction by the original scribe or by a contemporary 'whose writing is not distinguishable' from that of the original scribe. The reading is ἀδελφοῖς (to my brethren) for ὀφθαλμοῖς (with/to my eyes). Our suggestion is that the original reading was *le'ēnē 'eḥāy* (in the sight of my brethren), that the second word was lost, and that the rest of the verse was added by an early scribe who was perhaps not quite as good as he ought to have been, but certainly knew human nature. Chapter 31 now becomes Job's public statement on oath. This statement is what he is prepared to stand by in any court whatsoever. He prefaces his statement with a declaration of his own orthodox beliefs, and follows that with a claim that he has nothing to fear from a God who himself has seen and can test every statement. Thus vv. 5-34, 38-40 are the statement on oath which he will proudly bear (vv. 36f.), openly declaring his whole way of life.

But how are vv. 5-34 and 38-40 to be translated? Many of them begin with the conjunction (? particle) *'im*, the most common use of which is in conditional clauses where the condition is already or likely to be fulfilled. There is, however, another common use of this particle; it introduces the substance of an oath. The opening of the chapter suggests that here we are dealing with a series of statements made on oath. We regard the chapter as a series of such statements, interspersed with explanatory comments by the speaker. For instance, v. 9 is the statement on oath; v. 10 states what he is prepared to see happen if his statement is false; vv. 11 and 12 form a comment on such action.

> 9 I swear that
> My heart has not been enticed over a woman,
> And I have not lurked at my neighbour's door.
> 10 If so,
> Let my wife be under-rider to another,
> And let others bow down over her.
> 11 Indeed that would be a sin of unchastity;
> That is an offence punishable by the judges.
> 12 Indeed it is a fire that eats down to Abaddon,
> And destroys the roots of all my produce.

This avoids almost entirely the problem of apparent disarrangements within the chapter, a supposed situation which has led to so many differing suggestions that little confidence can be placed in any one of them. The multiplicity of answers suggests that the wrong question is being asked.

At the end of ch. 31 there is a note: 'the words of Job are ended'. This is a very strange statement. The natural meaning of it is that everything up to this point has been said by Job and that there is nothing more from him after this point. This latter is indeed the case, apart from the apology and the recantation in 40.3-5 and 42.2-6. The statement can be paralleled with a similar note at the end of Ps. 72: 'The prayers of David the son of Jesse are ended.' In its present position and considering the arrangement of the rest of the Psalter, the statement is doubly wrong. There are many non-Davidic psalms earlier, and there are Davidic psalms later: 86; 101; 103; 108; 109; 110; 122; 124; 131; 133; 138-45. In LXX there are still more Davidic psalms, following the general tendency of the latter part of the Hebrew Psalter and still more so of the LXX to ascribe a psalm to David when there is no note of this type in the Hebrew. Originally the words, 'to David', 'to Asaph', 'to the Choirmaster' or 'to the sons of Korah', signified that the psalm in question was taken from one of these earlier collections, but later the word appears to have been taken to signify authorship. Ewald asked himself the question whether there is any way in which the statement in Ps. 72.20 can be regarded as true, especially true both ways, so to speak—none but Davidic psalms before it and no Davidic psalms after it. There must be, thought he, some way in which the statement is true. Ewald's solution was concerned with the 'lonely' Asaph psalm, Ps. 50. He pointed out that if the Elohist psalms 51-72 followed the Yahwist psalms (1), 2-41, then we would have a whole series of Davidic psalms. This group would consist of (1), 2-41 (except perhaps 33) and 51-72 (the Solomon psalm being included), and it ends with the note which says that this is the end of the Davidic psalms. This would then be followed by a group of Korahite psalms, 42-49, and lastly by the Asaphite psalms with the lonely Ps. 50 now joined to its fellows, 73-83. These are followed by a miscellaneous group of Yahwist psalms, 84-89, and so we come to the end of Book Three of the Psalter, after which the method of compilation changes.[2] It will be seen that this proposal of Ewald's does three separate things. It restores the lonely Asaphite psalm to its companions; it brings all the Davidic psalms together (those, that is, in the first three books of the Psalter ; it ensures that the note at the end of Ps. 72 makes sense both ways: all Davidic before and no Davidic after.

Just as Ewald's suggestion made the phrase at the end of Ps. 72 full of meaning and all in a precise and exact way, so also by adopting a similar explanation, the phrase at the end of Job 31 can come to have a full and exact meaning. If we assume that in the first edition of Job, the three friends did not appear, nor Elihu, nor ch. 28, then the note means that everything up to this point has been spoken by Job and nothing after it, apart from the recantations. And further, nothing up to this point has been spoken by anybody else. Job's soliloquy consists of chs. 3; 29-31; each chapter of which is composed of and is devoted to one particular theme. The other speeches in the complete Job are not as clearly distinct from each other as these four chapters are, nor are they so self-contained, except for the separateness of ch. 28.

---

[2] For further details of the compilation of the Psalter, see N. H. Snaith, *The Psalms: a short introduction*, 1945, pp. 7-11; and 'The Triennial Cycle and the Psalter', *ZAW* X (1933), pp. 302-7.

Further, the four chapters of the soliloquy are different from the speeches of the dialogue proper. In these four chapters, 3 and 29-31, there is no argument and no discussion; no charges are made against God. We have: (1) ch. 3, Job's question: 'Why was I ever born?' (2) ch. 29, Job's previous state of prosperity and honour (3) ch. 30, Job's present state of humiliation and disgrace (4) ch. 31, Job's solemn oaths that he is completely innocent.

2. *Yahweh speeches*

We pass now to God's answer to Job, which is in two parts. It consists of chs. 38-39, followed by Job's humble apology in 40.3-5, and 40.6-41.26, followed by Job's abject submission. Chapters 38-39 contain a statement of God's almighty power as it is manifested in the natural world, first (ch. 38) in creation and in the maintaining of the ordered cosmos, and secondly (ch. 39) in the provision which he makes for those wild creatures which are by no means subordinate to the will of man. Man is wholly and completely unable to touch the fringe of these works of God which demand divine wisdom and efficiency.

(*a*) *Chapters* 38-39

There has been much discussion concerning the section which deals with the ostrich (39.13-18). The ancient versions found the word *rᵉnānīm* (39.13) difficult.[3] Many scholars regard the section as an interpolation, especially since it has been supplied to LXX from Th.[4] Possibly the bird is being described as senseless and cruel, but we do not think this is the case, since the quoting of the word *'akzār* (cruel) in Lam. 4.3 is valid only if it is first agreed that we must emend the text in Job 39.13. The whole section is actually saying that the bird, whatever it is, is a law to herself.

---

[3] Most assume that it involves the idea of 'loud cries, rejoicing, singing', deriving it from the root *rūn*: LXX (Th) τερπομένων, Aq αἰνούντων, Sym ἀγλαϊσμοῦ, S *sabbāḥin*. But T has 'prairie hen'. The 'peacocks' of AV goes back to V's *struthio*; so also DV, JB. Hoffmann and others read *yᵉʿēnim* (cf. the Qere in Lam. 4.3), which is held to mean 'voracious one'. Dhorme is sure the bird is an ostrich because of the details of vv. 14-18. Others say the word is equivalent to the more common *bᵉnōt yaʿᵃnā* (daughters of the desert), which LXX and V identify with the ostrich, but more likely they are some kind of owl. They and the *tannīm* (jackals: the rare Arabic *tīnān* is the wolf, Post) are mentioned in Isa. 34.13; 43.20 as types of loneliness and isolation.

[4] So Bickell, Duhm, Cheyne, Beer and others. Dillmann and Peake are doubtful.

She breaks all the rules of behaviour, including the role of caring for her own eggs. Indeed, the point of all the references to animals and other creatures in ch. 39 is that man can no more control them than he can control the mighty forces of the universe of ch. 38. It is because the critics have not realized this that they have been uneasy about the inclusion as genuine of this section in the book as (at any time) it left the author's hands. The whole point of the Yahweh speech in both chs. 38 and 39 is the limited capacity of man and his inability to control either earth and sea and sky or the wild animals. This is the common theme which makes the two chapters of this speech into a coherent whole.

The next section, 39.19-25, deals with the chariot horse. This is the only creature mentioned in these two chapters that is not wholly wild and untamed. The section certainly follows v. 18: 'she scorneth the horse and its driver' (not 'rider') and at first sight it may be thought to be an addition with a link-word *sūs* (chariot horse) in vv. 18f. But the point of the section is that as soon as the sound of battle is heard, nobody can control the warhorse, and it is this headlong, uncontrollable rush that makes him what he is. Viewed from this point of view, the war-horse is another example of the theme of the chapter: there are all these living creatures which man cannot control. Man is no more lord of the surface of the earth than he is lord of sea and sky. The inference is that all these things are subject to the control of God alone, and he is master also of the primeval ocean and of the giant forces of nature. We regard, therefore, the whole of chs. 38 and 39 as belonging to the first edition of Job.

Chapter 38 deals first with the power and knowledge of God manifest in creation and in all natural phenomena from highest and farthest heaven to the realms of the dead. Then (v. 39) it turns to wild animals and continues with them into the next chapter.

In ch. 39 the author continues with descriptions of various creatures which man cannot control: the wild goat, the wild ass, the wild ox, the ostrich, the war-horse, and he ends with the birds of prey. This speech continues into 40.2, and is followed by Job's apology, 40.3-5.

Many scholars rightly emphasize the excellence of this speech of Yahweh's (chs. 38-39 and 40.2). Indeed J. T. Marshall[5] is so impressed by its high literary standard that he ascribes it on that

[5] *Job and his Comforters*, 1904, p. 6.

ground to another author. Driver-Gray[6] retain this first speech
though at one time they were inclined to deny both speeches
chs. 38-39 and 40.6-41.3 to the original author. We do not find
that the literary style is markedly different from that of the soliloquy (chs. 3; 29-31). We find indeed common characteristics in
the soliloquy, the dialogue proper (chs. 4-27) and this Yahweh
speech; the marked tendency to use a word in its original as well
as in its developed sense, the care taken to ensure proper couplets
(but without the over-care of the Elihu speeches), and the tendency to elaborate a simile and continue with it, introducing
details which have nothing to do with the object for which the
simile was introduced.

This first Yahweh speech is followed by an apology from Job,
who admits (40.4-5) that he is of no account and has nothing to
say in reply. He covers his mouth with his hand. He has spoken
once; he will not say another word. This is an apology for ever
having said anything, and an acknowledgment that he has nothing
to say in reply to all Yahweh's questions in chs. 38-39. But it is
not submission. This comes later, after the second Yahweh
speech.

(b) 40.6-41.34

This second speech begins at 40.7, and from v. 7 to v. 14 Job
is being asked, possibly ironically, possibly not, to assume the
necessary power and to instruct God to do what Job says he
ought to do: bring low the proud and pull down the wicked.
God says: if you can do it, then by all means do it; and I will give
you the praise.

Then we get a description of a monster called Behemoth
(40.15-24), and this is followed in 40.25-41.26 (EVV, 41.1-34)
with the description of another monster named Leviathan. These
are creatures whose characteristic is enormous strength, and they
have this much in common with the uncontrollable creatures of
the first Yahweh speech: no man can control them.

But who or what is Behemoth?[7] The word is an intensive

---

[6] *Job*, p. lxiii.
[7] LXX (θηρία) translates the Hebrew word as an ordinary plural (wild
beasts), and so also T, but V and S transliterate. DV, AV and RV all have
'Behemoth' in the text, but AVm identifies it with the elephant, and RVm
with the hippopotamus. JB suggests that Behemoth stands for the typical

plural[8] and means 'the greatest of beasts', 'the Great Beast' or
'*The* Beast'. Two solutions are offered. One is that the author is
thinking of the hippopotamus, and the other that the beast is the
mythical sea-monster, the sea-dragon of the ancient creation myth.
In seventh-century BC Babylon she was called Tiamat; in Israel
she was Rahab; at Ugarit she was Yam the sea.[9] It is indeed true
that the creatures described in these two chapters differ in type
from the creatures of the first Yahweh speech, but this does not
necessarily involve them in being mythical creatures. The aim is
different. The earlier creatures (those of the first Yahweh speech)
are examples of wild, untamed creatures which man cannot control. The creatures of the second speech are marvellous creatures
which God alone can create, creatures which scarcely any of the
readers have seen, and of which they have heard only strange and
wondrous tales. The first group is intended to emphasize the
weakness and lack of wisdom and the inefficiency of man. The
second group is to demonstrate the incomparable power of a God
who could so create and can so control.

In each case, there are details concerning Behemoth and
Leviathan which suggest an actual beast which we know. The
first is the hippopotamus, and the second is the crocodile.
Behemoth eats grass and is of great strength and vigour. He lies
beneath the lotus plants and among the reeds in the marsh. This
is the hippopotamus. Given that the beast was unknown in the
author's country, heard of in travellers' tales, given also that
many, many centuries later everybody believed in the existence of
unicorns and hippographs, given also the tales of huge sea-
monsters which frightened the sixteenth- and seventeenth-century
sailors, and finally, granted that the author is a poet of no mean
ability and imagination, long since given to expanding his illustrations and making short excursuses of them—granted all this,
we see nothing here that cannot be understood as being descriptive of the hippopotamus of African rivers and lakes. After all,
even Herodotus never got beyond the cataract at Assouan; and
he can tell strange tales.

Similarly, in the case of Leviathan, there are many details which

---

'beast' or 'brute', and that the origin may well be the Egyptian *pehemu*, the
ox of the waters.

[8] GK, 124*a, e, i.*

[9] The full case for this mythological identification is in H. Gunkel, *Schöpfung
und Chaos im Urzeit und Endzeit,* 2nd ed., 1921, pp. 41-49.

suggest the crocodile. Allowing for all the same factors as before, travellers' tales and so forth, and once more remembering strange tales of strange beasts very much nearer our own time, Moby Dick, the giant squid, the great sea-serpent, the Loch Ness monster, there is nothing here incompatible with the author's imaginative ideas of what a crocodile is.[10] Reference is made in the commentaries, particularly by S. Terrien,[11] to frescoes in ancient Egypt in which the hippopotamus and the crocodile are portrayed side by side, and indeed sometimes fighting.[12] These frescoes remind us forcibly of the lion and the unicorn of the British Coat of Arms. There never was a lion quite like that, and there never was a unicorn at all. There never was a hippopotamus quite like Behemoth, nor was there ever a crocodile like Leviathan. But in the memory of a man who has faced either or both, himself armed with only spear or bow and arrow, by the time he had stopped running, and even more when he had told the story many times, the hippopotamus was like Behemoth and the crocodile was all that he says of Leviathan. The two beasts are indeed the hippopotamus and the crocodile, perhaps invested with heraldic elements, perhaps with elements from whatever myth the Egyptian frescoes portray, but certainly with all the wonder elements of travellers' tales. The weakness of Gunkel's mythological theory is that there is not enough of the myth and far too much of the actual creatures we know. There could so very easily have been so very much more of the myth. The fact that both names have been used for the mythical sea-monster, even though the name 'leviathan' may have a pre-history of this nature, means that others have sought to do before him what Gunkel did.

We see no sufficient reason for denying these two chapters to the original author or to the first edition of the Book of Job. We say this partly because we do not find enough evidence to warrant denying them to him, and partly because Job has not yet submitted to the divine will. He has regretted having spoken, and he has said he has no more to say, but he has not

---

[10] See photographs of hippopotamuses and crocodiles such as those taken by Des Bartlett in Collins' *Animals of Africa* series, *The Rivers and Lakes* (Armand Denis), especially the photograph of the crocodile on p. 5 and those of hippopotamuses later in the volume.

[11] *IB*, III, p. 1186.

[12] Cf. A. Erman, *Life in Ancient Egypt*, ET, 1894, pp. 239f. See also the late tomb of Petosiris.

humbly submitted to God's overpowering wisdom and might.

Job's submission is embedded in the confused verses in ch. 42 which are the conclusion of the poetic part of Job.[13] So the poem as it comes down to us ends with a humble and repentant apology and the way is opened for the *dénouement* of the epilogue, with Job's friends and relations all crowding round him to congratulate him in his renewed prosperity.

Thus the first draft (edition) of the Book of Job consisted of four parts:

1. The prologue (1.1-2.10) and the epilogue (42.9c-17), but omitting the phrase 'when he prayed for his friend'.
2. Job's soliloquy (3; 29-31).
3. Yahweh's reply (38-39) followed by Job's apology (40.1-5).
4. Yahweh's further reply (40.6-41.34) followed by Job's abject submission (42.2, 3c, 5, 6).

[13] Compare 42.3ab with 38.2, the opening of the first Yahweh speech: 38.2 has the root *ḥšk* (be dark) and 42.3 has the root *'lm* I (conceal), but one Hebrew MS (Kennicott 100) actually has the root *ḥšk* in 42.3; LXX and S add 'with words' (*bᵉmillin*) in 42.3, and in general LXX makes use of 38.2 in its rendering of 42.3. LXX certainly is assimilating, but the process has already begun in the Hebrew text. It is difficult to see how lines 3ab can properly belong to 42.3. Similarly the whole of verse 4 is an interpolation: cf. 21.2f.; 33.31; 38.3b; notice also the emphatic 'I'.

IV

THE FIRST CYCLE OF SPEECHES: CHAPTERS 3-13

THE three friends appear at 2.11, Eliphaz from Teman, Bildad from Shuah and Zophar from Naamah. They come in quite suddenly, as suddenly as Elihu, for there is nothing previous to 2.11 which would lead one to expect their appearance. Teman is at the northern end of Edom (Ezek. 25.13). According to Gen. 25.2, Shuah was a son of Keturah and the sixth son she bore to Abraham. According to Gen. 25.3 (LXX). Sheba, Teman and Dedan were sons of Kokshan who was Shuah's brother. Zophar's traditional home is uncertain. There was a *Naʿᵃmā* in the Philistine country (Josh. 15.41). But this can scarcely be the place intended. According to I Chron. 4.15, there was a *Naʿam* in the Calebite area near Hebron. *Naʿam* was the third son of Caleb. This is more likely to be the place-tribe intended, and thus the homes of all the three friends are in Edom, or at least well within the Negeb. The Edomite tradition is strong in the supplement at the end of the book, according to the LXX. There Job is identified with Jobab and thus is a king of Edom, the successor of Balak, son of Beor. He lived on the boundaries of Idumea and Arabia and he married an Arabian wife. His father was Zare, one of the sons of Esau, though according to the Hebrew of Gen. 36.13, this Zerah was the second son of Reuel, son of Esau. Reuel was the second son and Eliphaz the first, but by a different wife. Through his mother, Bosorra, he was fifth from Abraham. The three of them were kings, though Zophar is a 'tyrant'. Driver-Gray[1] think of the Minaean colony of El-ʿola, which is in Arabia, some 400 miles south of Gaza and some 800 miles north of Sana. The Sophar of LXX is an Edomite, allied with Eliphaz and Teman (Gen. 16.11, 15; I Chron. 1. 36) and Eliphaz is an Edomite (Gen. 36.10f.; I Chron. 1.35f.). The Job of the Hebrew text is one of the great ones, a prince of the sons of the East. In LXX, he is a king of Edom, and the three friends are all kings of Orient. The

[1] *Job*, p. xxviii.

45

archaic setting of the tale grows with the years, both in wealth of detail and in the legendary greatness of the characters. Probably the author picked out these Edomite names to give colour to his picture of antiquity.

1. *Chapters* 4-5

These two chapters comprise the first speech of Eliphaz. The speech is a short summary of the orthodox position concerning suffering. God prospers the righteous, but brings the wicked to utter disaster. God knows best and he works out his sovereign will. If an innocent man meets with trouble, he should accept it with patient endurance, knowing that in the end it will work out for his greater good. No mortal man can ever be in the right (? come out on top) as against God. God depends upon no one, neither on earth beneath nor in heaven above. Therefore there is nobody who can help a man against God. A man stands no chance at all of getting a verdict against God. Further, no man has any right to blame God for his troubles. Every man makes his own, and all the more so if he gets vexed when things go wrong. All that a man can do is to cast himself on God's mercy, because God does indeed lift up the fallen and the helpless, and he does indeed bring disaster to all who think they are wiser than he is and set themselves up against him. Eliphaz's only solution is absolute and complete submission.

2. *Chapter* 6

This chapter contains Job's reply to Eliphaz; that is, if the speech is a reply in any proper sense of the word, and not a speech of the opposition, regardless of what has been said immediately before in the debate. Job says that it is no wonder he is full of vexation. This is, of course, the Job of the dialogue, and not the Job of the prologue or of the soliloquy. The Job of the prologue and of the soliloquy is patient and submissive (1.21; 2.10). He does not complain, but patiently accepts his fate. Not so, this Job of the dialogue. Here he says that he has suffered so very, very much. Why does not God finish him off altogether and have done with it? Job's friend has disappointed him and has given him no sort of comfort.

3. *Chapter* 7

This chapter is the opening speech in the second phase of the first cycle. This phase consists of three speeches: Job, Bildad, Job. Here in ch. 7 the author is back on the old theme, though here Job is sharing the common lot of all mankind (7.1, 2). Job gives up and wants to die. The life of mortal man is hard, but his is harder than most. Why does God give man such a bad time? It cannot matter to the High God what feeble man does. Why does not God pardon Job and have done with it?

4. *Chapter* 8

This chapter contains Bildad's speech in the second phase of the first cycle of speeches. It consists of a straight denial of Job's charge that God is unjust, though actually it is by no means clear that Job at this stage had actually gone so far as to make this charge against God. In any case, says Bildad, Job need not fear. He must make his appeal to God. If he is pure and upright, and if he is earnest in his intercession, then God will intervene on his behalf and will put everything right, thus ensuring great prosperity for Job. This virtually is what indeed does happen in the epilogue where all is doubly well after Job has acknowledged his fault in even speaking at all.

5. *Chapter* 9

In this chapter we have Job's reply to Bildad. Job says that no man can possibly win his case against God who is incomparable in power. Job knows himself to be innocent, but he would find himself on the losing side as soon as he opened his mouth. God makes no distinction between the innocent and the guilty. This is because the verdict in this world is controlled by power and not necessarily by what is right. Indeed, the effect of all this is that God seems to be on the side of the wicked. In any case, why should God go to all the trouble he has taken in making man and preserving him, only to treat him like this?

6. *Chapter* 10

This chapter opens in much the same way as ch. 7 which we took to be the opening speech in the second phase of the first cycle, a phase which consisted of three speeches: Job, Bildad, Job. In the same way, we take ch. 10 to be the opening speech by Job in the third phase of the first cycle. Why should God maintian this severe watch on Job? Apparently all the time that God was

nourishing him and making him develop, there was this anta-
gonism lurking in the background. Job ends by appealing for a
short time of relief before he passes on, out into the darkness,
never to return.

7. *Chapter* 11

This chapter contains Zophar's speech in the first cycle. At
first sight it seems to be somewhat short, but actually it is only
one and a half couplets shorter than Bildad's speech in ch. 8.
This speech in ch. 11 is wholly concerned with maintaining the
orthodox position. Whatever Job says is nothing but words and
words and words. If God were to speak to him, then he (Job)
would understand that there is no real problem. The old orthodoxy still stands. If Job is innocent, all will be well. If Job is not
innocent, then let him turn over a new leaf and then all will be
abundantly well. Job need have no fears and no doubts whatsoever.

8. *Chapter* 12

We take this chapter and the next to belong to the third phase
of the first cycle and to constitute Job's reply to Zophar. We take
ch. 14 to be the opening speech, Job's opening speech, in the
second cycle. Commentators have found difficulties in both chs.
12 and 13, and some have assumed that there have been large
interpolations.[2] But if we recognize that the author is fond of
and prone to little excursuses and digressions, then the arguments in favour of interpolations are not so strong. Here in this
chapter Job flatly denies that the three friends know what they
are talking about. He says that the facts are the exact opposite of
what they say. God has no consideration for any man, and nobody
can stand against him. Not even the great ones of earth can op-
pose him: kings, counsellors, judges, priests, whole nations—all
alike are helpless, and Job's friends more than any.

9. *Chapter* 13

This chapter begins equally bluntly and almost as rudely as
the previous chapter. In the first nineteen verses Job is speaking
to the three friends, but from v. 20 onwards he addresses himself

---

[2] Grill, for instance, omits 12.4-13.2; Siegfried omits 12.4-13.1; Driver-
Gray regard 12.2-12 as largely an addition.

to God. 13.2b is exactly the same as 12.3b, which is perhaps an interpolation there from 13.2b, but since there is a doubt about some verses in ch. 12, and since 13.1ff. bears many signs of the beginning of a speech, it may well be that the whole of chapter 12 is an amateurish alternative for, or a possible replacement of, ch. 13.

In this first cycle of speeches (3-13) the three friends have all been perfectly orthodox. They are quite sure that God is just and righteous and that if Job appeals to him, he can and will speedily make all abundantly well. Of all this they have no slightest doubt. Job also is orthodox to the extent that he also believes that God is just, but he has his problems. Theory and fact do not obviously fit; perhaps they do not fit at all. Job's friends have done nothing but repeat the old orthodoxy, but for Job this simply will not do. The old orthodoxy and the traditional statement of it do not fit the facts of experience. Job believes that justice should not merely be said to be done, but that, both from heaven and on earth, it should be seen to be done. So far as Job can see, men suffer indiscriminately. This is because God is so far removed in excellence and distance that there is no contact. The only variation from this is that sometimes God appears to be more against one group than against another. Sometimes he is against the underprivileged, and the arrogant and greedy man prospers. Sometimes God is regarded as being more against those of high estate than against those of low degree. This is because those in high estate are more prone to *hubris* (the classical Hebrew example is Isa. 14.13f.), and therefore tend in thought and in private ambition, if not always in deliberate action, to threaten the unique position of the High God.

V

THE SECOND CYCLE OF SPEECHES:
14.1-21.21

THE second cycle of speeches begins, according to our view, with the speech of Job in ch. 14, and it continues into ch. 21. The general opinion is that the second cycle concludes at the end of ch. 21. But ch. 21 is of inordinate length for one chapter, though not long enough for two. There is a definite break at the end of v.21, and this fits in with the general trend in the dialogue, according to which things tend to get shorter as the dialogue continues. At v. 22 the speaker turns away from discussing the untoward prosperity of the wicked man, and he begins a new topic. He turns once again to the problem of the incidence of suffering, as he has previously done in the first speech of a phase: 7.1; 10.1; 14.1; 17.1. Sometimes he speaks of the suffering of mankind, and sometimes of his own suffering, but in each case he is beginning again, just as in 3.3. Here in 21.22 his topic is, as Dhorme says,[1] 'death strikes at random'. The incidence of death and suffering is indiscriminate. We therefore think (though not with the same confidence as in the first phase) that the third phase of the second cycle (i.e. of the second cycle as a whole) ends at 21.21, and that the third cycle begins at 21.22. Similarly, there is a break in ch. 19 at the end of verse 22, so that the third phase may well begin at 19.22. But the pattern is beginning to fade in the middle of the second cycle. It fades out altogether in the so-called third cycle, and all are agreed about this, since they try to construct such a pattern.

1. Chapter 14

In this chapter, Job meditates on the shortness and the uncertainty of human life. Thus the phase begins similarly to the way in which the phases of the first cycle begins: 3.3; 7.1; 10.1. Here in ch. 14 the picture is of a tree cut down or of a deciduous tree (14.8). The tree will sprout again when it gets the first scent

[1] E. Dhorme, *A Commentary on the Book of Job*, ET, 1967, p. 318.

of water. But man is not like that. When he is cut down, he withers, and that is the end of him. He does not come back again. And then (v. 13) Job has a sudden thought and a hope. What if ...? What if a man could hide underground—not die and be buried, but just hide—and there be kept concealed and safe until the trouble be over?[2] He could be given a fixed time to lie low, and then, when God called him, Job could answer, however long he had had to wait. If only this could happen. But it is too much to hope for; man decays and passes by, just as everything else does.

2. *Chapter* 15

This chapter contains Eliphaz's speech in the first phase of the second cycle. Here he changes somewhat his attitude to Job. He says now that Job has condemned himself out of his own mouth, he has turned against God. Eliphaz then restates the old orthodox position, based on tradition. The wicked man meets with disaster and he dies before his time.

3. *Chapter* 16

Commentators see here a change of attitude on the part of Job, but whatever change there is, is in ch. 16, Job's reply to Eliphaz. The change is not in ch. 17, which we regard as the opening speech of the second phase: the Job, Bildad, Job sequence. The commentators say that Job is now appealing, so to speak, to God against God—appealing to a God of impartial and strict justice against a God who is flagrantly unjust in his dealings with men. This assumes that God is the arbiter of 16.19, but we do not find this to be so. Rather, Job is thinking of the 'daysman' of 9.33, the umpire who could put his hand on both God and Job and see fair play. The author is faced with the dilemma of a world in which for the most part injustice rules and God is believed to be both righteous and just. But justice is not even done on earth, let alone seen to be done. Job is hoping for some supernatural being or for some sort of personalized rightness which can deal with a High God who, if there is any true monotheism, must also in some way be the prince of this world. The chapter opens with

[2] The 'again' of AV, RV, RSV in 14.14 is not in the Hebrew. We understand the verse to mean: if a man 'dies', can he revive again as a deciduous tree does?

the normal tirade against the previous speaker (vv. 1-8), this being the normal way in which the author works and the concession he makes to his dialogue framework.

4. *Chapter* 17

Here Job starts again. Once more he is concerned with his own particular sad lot. Each phase opens either with the sad lot of mankind in general or with the sad lot of Job in particular. The chapter is unremarkable. It says nothing that has not been said by Job before, though now with other phrases and similes. Verses 8-10 seem to be out of place. The best suggestion by which the verses can be retained here is that of Terrien.[3] He thinks the verses can be retained if we understand Job to be referring to himself as an example or encouragement to future sufferers. Let the upright look at this (what is happening to me) and be astounded: here is the example of a righteous man holding on to his way. Perhaps when men see this, they will be strengthened to endure. At first sight such sentiments do not seem to be true to the character of Job, but there is no great force in this objection, since the author attributes many ideas to Job, and certainly the Job of the dialogue is very different indeed from the Job of the prologue. But in spite of this explanation, vv. 8-9 still look like an intrusion and v. 10 is difficult.

5. *Chapter* 18

In his reply Bildad complains that Job treats his friends with contempt. He then goes on to reiterate the old orthodox ideas. The wicked must of necessity come to a bad end. The subject of the chapter is old and it all has been said before, but many of the couplets in this chapter are quite elegant in literary style and the illustrations are picturesque.

6. 19.1-22

Job's reply to Bildad is in ch. 19, but we do not find a speech for the opening of the third phase; not, that is, in a convincing manner, but there is a break at the end of v. 22, and perhaps the opening speech of the third phase may begin at 19.23. Whatever Job has said in his previous speeches, he certainly accuses God in this chapter of being hostile to him. The friends are no better than God; both he and they persecute Job.

[3] *IB*, III, pp. 1031f.

7. 19.23-29

The character of the contents of ch. 19 change entirely at the end of v. 22. Up to this point Job has been accusing God of active and continued hostility against him, but from v. 23 onwards the situation is entirely different. He now says that he is quite sure that as and when he sees God, then God will be on his side, and he himself full of joy. We translate vv. 25-27b as follows:

> I myself know that my vindicator is alive,
> And by and by he will stand up on the ground.
> At the last a witness[4] will be raised up by my side,[5]
> And in my joy[6] I shall see God.
> I shall see him myself;
> My own eyes, and no stranger's, shall behold him.

The problem all the time is God's remoteness and his absenteeism. This is what has led to the apparent abandonment of Job, and it is the cause of all that has happened to him. It is not that God is unjust. That is not what is causing the trouble. It is that he is remote. Here is the perpetual problem of the High God. The High God is altogether too high, too remote to be concerned with the affairs of men.

8. *Chapter* 20

Here is Zophar's speech in the third phase of the second cycle. The author by this time is running short of what can be said in favour of the orthodox position. Indeed, he is not finding it easy to provide Job with enough to say in a three-cycle dialogue. Evidently the author has been committed, willy-nilly, to this three-cycle dialogue within prose prologue and epilogue. It is the pattern demanded by the kind of writing in which he is engaged. He is halfway through his programme, but he is finding it quite difficult to maintain. Chapter 20 contains nothing new. We have the same appeal to ancient tradition and once more a reiteration of orthodox belief. This time: it may be that the wicked man triumphs, but the duration of his triumph is short. Quickly and completely he will be brought to complete disaster.

[4] Read *weʾaḥēr ʿēdī* (and later, my witness), Bickell, Duhm.
[5] Read *yizzādēp ʾittī* (will be raised up with me), Richter. The root is *zqp* (lift up), Accadian, Aramaic, Syriac.
[6] We propose reading a noun *beśer* (joy), cf. Arabic *baśira*, Ugarit *bśr* (B IV 3.34, etc.). The Hebrew verb *biśśer* means 'gladden the heart with good tidings' and *beśōrā* means 'good tidings'.

9. 21.1-21

Job's reply to Zophar is found in 21.1-21, and this completes the third phase of the second cycle of speeches; that is, it completes the second cycle itself. But these verses are difficult, and contrary statements are found in them. From v.22 all is well, and vv.22-34 are readily attributable to Job. After the usual preliminary couplets (vv. 2-3), the speaker says that the friends ought to be astonished at what has happened. When he himself thinks back, he is amazed. Then (vv. 7-15) we get a declaration in the true style of Job, saying that the wicked do indeed prosper in this world, and this is in spite of their wickedness and in spite of the fact that they ignore God completely. Verses 16-22 are difficult, because, as they stand, they are contrary to Job's opinions and experience as stated elsewhere. They speak of the deserved misfortunes of the wicked rich, and as they stand in the Hebrew, they can more naturally be attributed to one or other of the three friends.[7]

10. 21.22-26

Here we get an absolute denial of the soundness of the orthodox views of the aged and the wise. We understand this to be Job's opening speech in the third cycle.

[7] The anomaly of vv. 16-22 was noticed as early as LXX. The Greek translators sought to solve the difficulty by omitting the negative in v. 16. This certainly is an effective way of dealing with this, or any other difficulty, but it is of doubtful legitimacy. V makes the speaker hope that he may be far removed from the counsel of the wicked, 'because (DV) their good things are not in their hand'. This does not make the verse suitable for Job, since all along he has been maintaining that their good things are in their hand. The anomalies, therefore, still remain in V and DV, and also in AV and RV. RSV turns the line into a question, and so also does JB, but RVm suggests the insertion of 'ye say'. It is plain that if vv. 16-22 are to be retained as an integral part of a speech of Job's, one or other of these expedients must be adopted. Merx followed LXX and omitted the negative. Beer was in favour either of omitting the negative or of making the line a question. Evidently he found as much, or as little, justification for the one as for the other. But the difficulty does not end with v. 16. The same treatment must be applied to v. 17, to v. 18, and so on through to v. 22. We certainly must insert 'You say' at the beginning of v. 19. The best solution (if, that is, we are determined to retain these verses as genuinely spoken by Job) is to insert 'You say' at the beginning of v. 16, since in any case we have to do this for v. 19a; let the interrogative of v. 17a continue through to the end of v. 18. Then v. 19b-21 can be treated as Job's caustic comments on orthodox opinion in that it has had to abandon its first line of defence, which is that the wicked man pays the full penalty himself, and has had to fall back on a second line of defences 'Well: it falls on his sons.'

VI

THE SO-CALLED THIRD CYCLE OF SPEECHES
21.22-27.23

THE so-called third cycle of speeches begins, in our view, at
21.22. But chs. 22-27 can scarcely be called a third cycle at all.
The pattern of the first and the second cycles is not followed
except partially and to a definitely limited extent. Chapter 22 is
ascribed to Eliphaz, and chs. 23 and 24 to Job; 25 to Bildad and
26 to Job. But here the pattern changes. Chapter 27 is ascribed
to Job but as an additional speech. The introductory verse reads:
'and Job added to lift up his parable (*māšāl*) and said'. This is the
way in which ch. 29 begins, a chapter which is generally recognized as being outside the dialogue. At the very least, the unusual
beginning of ch. 27 is 'a further indication of the disturbed state
of the text' (Terrien). Some, like Fohrer, regard the line either as
a redactionary substitution for a normal opening or as an insertion consequent upon dislocation. As things stand, chs. 27 and 28
belong together as an additional speech by Job, but most scholars
agree that ch. 28, the so-called Wisdom Poem, is a separate piece,
distinct from the rest.

In this so-called third cycle we have rather more than one half
of a normal cycle. We have a short speech by Job (21.22-34), and
then speeches by Eliphaz (ch. 22) and Job (ch. 23); then a speech
by Job (ch. 24), a short speech by Bildad (ch. 25) and a speech by
Job (ch. 26). There is no speech by Zophar, and, if ch. 27 is indeed different, there is no speech by Job either before or after the
missing speech by Zophar. Was there ever a third cycle? Is it
necessary to try to reconstitute the third phase of this so-called
third cycle? For, according to our reckoning, while both phase
one and phase two are shorter in length than those in the previous
two cycles, it is the third phase that is missing.

But there are difficulties in this so-called third cycle almost from
the beginning. Job's introductory speech (21.22-34) is satisfactory
enough as the opening of the first phase of a third cycle. There is
a new element in the speech—death comes indiscriminately—but

a new approach is entirely proper for the new phase. The difficulties begin with ch. 22. This speech is ascribed to Eliphaz, but there are elements here very different from anything which has previously been put into Eliphaz's mouth. In his first speech he was truly orthodox. God is just and righteous. The world is run that way, and he runs it. He is against the crafty and arrogant, but he saves the poor and needy. It is true that he sometimes inflicts wounds, but he heals and binds them up. Eliphaz does not accuse Job of sinning or of rebelling against God. Job can safely trust in a righteous Saviour-God. In his second speech (ch. 15) Eliphaz has much less patience. He accuses Job of *hubris*, that arrogance against God which the Greek tragedians held to be the main cause of human woe. Eliphaz repeats the orthodox theory concerning the doom of the wicked. This-and-this is what happens to the man who tilts against God. Chapter 22 is different. Some scholars have seen in this chapter a climax in the development of Eliphaz's attitude to Job from true sympathy to downright harshness. Our judgment is that the situation in ch. 22 is markedly different. The speaker roundly accuses Job of being a desperate sinner, guilty of each and every sin and crime in the Deuteronomic calendar (vv. 6-9). He has taken security from a brother for a loan that amounts to next to nothing. He has taken the poor man's only cloak as a pledge and left him naked. He has not given water to the thirsty, nor food to the hungry. He has sent widows away empty-handed and has left the fatherless helpless. Job's wickedness has indeed been very great, and there is no end to his iniquity. This is why (v. 10) there are snares all round about him and traps in his path. Eliphaz calls on Job to repent and be humble. Conditionally upon this, he promises light and peace at last.

A further difference between this speech and the others is that whereas in the other two cycles Eliphaz opens with introductory couplets, more or less polite, but always giving the speeches a semblance of a dialogue, here there is nothing of the kind. In the previous two cycles there are preliminary couplets at the beginning of both the Eliphaz speeches, as is proper if (as we think) these speeches are in reply to a short speech from Job at the opening of the phase. Here in ch. 22. Eliphaz plunges straight into what he has to say, and the same thing is true of Bildad's speech in ch. 25.

Yet again, some elements in this Eliphaz speech (ch. 22) have raised doubts in the minds of scholars, and much of the speech has been regarded as a series of interpolations. For instance, Eliphaz's condemnation of Job is in vv. 5-9, but within this section there is the strange couplet of v. 8. It is not easy to see how this verse fits in with the surrounding verses.[1] One way of dealing with a recalcitrant verse is to turn it into a question, but while doubtless in some cases this is legitimate,[2] it is by no means a satisfying solution. There is a danger of such a solution being the last refuge of the defeated. After all, it is the equivalent of inserting a negative or of omitting a negative without any supporting evidence in any of the ancient versions, and largely on the basis of 'this *must* be so'. It can be a decidedly high-handed policy, and if it has to be done with any frequency, then it is better to check one's premisses. There may be another solution, depending on different premisses. Dhorme regards the verse as a sequel to Job's alleged actions. 'And the man of brute force got the land! And the favourite was settled on it!'—an admirable suggestion.

To continue: RVm has turned v. 11 into a question: 'Dost thou not see the darkness and the flood of waters that covereth thee?' This is based on an attempt of the Syriac (*Peshitta*) version to make sense of the verse, but it is a silly question. Peake says that the question makes little sense, since the one thing above all others of which Job has been conscious from the beginning is the darkness of his outlook and the veritable sea of troubles overwhelming him. Duhm thought v. 12 to be a gloss. LXX omits vv. 13-16. Peake thinks that vv. 17f. break the connection between 16 and 19. So also Budde and Duhm. Merx and Siegfried object to v. 18. Gray thinks that vv. 27f. are an intrusion into the original. Dillmann disliked v. 20. LXX omits v. 24, while Bickell and Duhm omit vv. 24f. Peake has grave doubts about v. 25 and there are also doubts about vv. 29f. These are samples of the diversity of opinion which is to be found in the commentaries. All have doubts and difficulties. There certainly are elements in ch. 22 which are true to the character of Eliphaz and to his attitude as it is portrayed in the previous cycles, but there are elements which cannot be so reconciled. Indeed, some elements are not easily

---

[1] Siegfried, Budde, Gray and Peake all regard it as being out of place.
[2] See *GK* 150a and *b*.

fitted into the framework of the sentiments of any of the four speakers.

Chapter 23 fits in well with what Job has been saying in previous speeches. He is still maintaining that if he can come face to face with God, he will get justice, but he also says that whichever way he turns, he can see no likelihood of this ever taking place. God acts far too autocratically for this. Job has no chance whatever, but he makes it quite clear that this is not going to silence him.

It is in ch. 24 that the problem reaches its most acute stage. All of it is markedly different from ch. 23. Merx in 1871 thought that the chapter is a substitute for a speech of Job's in which he was so wholly antagonistic to God that it was deemed too irreligious to be preserved. This is a curious suggestion, and it is still more curious that so many have accepted it, since 42.7 is already difficult enough without adding anything more to any speech of Job's of a doubtfully religious nature. Why should it be suggested that Job has graduated from unorthodoxy to blasphemy? Even comparatively conservative critics like Peake and Gray find much in this chapter which is alien to the Job of other speeches.

With respect to the poetic form of the chapter: there is certainly a number of three-line stanzas in the chapter as it has come down to us: vv. 5(?), 12, 13, 14, 15, 16, 18, 20 and 24, while vv. 17 and 19 are overloaded. It is true that elsewhere in the Book of Job we find three-line stanzas instead of the regular two-line couplet of 3:3 metre. But these sporadic three-line stanzas, assuming, that is, that some at least of them are original, may very well have been introduced, perhaps unconsciously but more likely deliberately, in order to provide an occasional but welcome variant to break up what would otherwise be a continuous and ultimately wearisome stream of 3:3 couplets. Even Virgil occasionally breaks the regular flow of hexameters with a short line. But in ch. 24 three-line stanzas appear to be the norm from v. 12 onwards. Indeed, Bickell and Duhm found the chapter to be composed exclusively of three-line stanzas. Merx found two sets of three-line stanzas, beginning with a couplet in v. 9 and another couplet in v. 17. Hoffmann thought that vv. 13-24 (which includes almost all the three-line stanzas) did not belong here at all, but were part of Bildad's speech. There are eight (? nine) three-line stanzas in this chapter. We estimate the number of three-line stanzas to be found in the Book of Job earlier than ch. 24 to be seventeen (? eighteen): 3.9; 4.16; 4.19; 6.4; 6.10(?); 7.11; 8.6; 9.24; 10.3; 10.15; 10.17; 10.22; 14.7; 14.12; 14.13; 15.28; 19.12; 21.17.

With regard to the contents of ch. 24, the first part consists of those charges of misgovernment, deliberate or through absenteeism, which are a feature of earlier speeches by Job. In fact, the charges here are not so much of mismanagement as of no management at all. There may be, even in these first few verses, a certain amount of dislocation (i.e. assuming an original coherent whole), but the pressure to admit this is not severe until v. 9 which is more akin to vv. 2-4 than to its present neighbours. The real crisis comes with v. 19, though Budde found himself in difficulties before this when he proposed to put v. 12 after v. 14b, and v. 14a before v. 16. Otherwise Budde felt that he could allow the whole chapter to Job without much difficulty. But vv. 18-21, in our view, scarcely express Job's sentiments as we know them from elsewhere. Many scholars have therefore thought that they must be quotations by Job of what the others have said.[3] Even Peake found himself forced to regard these four verses as alien elements, and the same applies to vv. 9 and 24. Verse 22a agrees with Job's general attitude, and so does v. 23, but this cannot be said of vv. 22b, 24 and 25. Duhm, as usual, is militantly thorough. He considers vv. 1-24 to belong to a series of poems which include also 12.4-6 and 30.2-8. Compare, in this respect, more recently Fohrer. The apparent diversity of the chapter led Bickell to think that vv. 5-8 and 10-12 do not belong here. Similarly, Grill omitted vv. 5-9 and 14-21. Siegfried considered vv. 13-24 to be a substitution, and in this he followed Merx. The Jerusalem Bible boldly transfers vv. 18acb to the end of ch. 27. Thus from all sides we see that here in ch. 24, as in ch. 22 in Eliphaz's third speech but to a greater extent, there are many elements which raise grave doubts whether it is proper to speak at all in terms of a third cycle of speeches.

Some scholars have sought to resolve the difficulties of ch. 24 by considering it in close connection with chs. 25-27, and even in connection with ch. 28 and with subsequent chapters. This desire to extend the discussion beyond ch. 27 is due to the fact that, whatever we do with chs. 22-27, there is not enough material in them to make anything like a proper cycle of speeches com-

---

[3] RV and RSV have followed this approach by inserting 'Ye say'.

parable with the other two, whatever rearrangements are proposed. In the first cycle (3-13) there are 277 verses; in the second
cycle (14.1-21.21) there are 195 verses; in chapters 21.22-27.23
there are 128 verses. All these figures include the introductory
verses.[4] Perhaps this continued decrease is acceptable, though
such figures as 128 or 115 makes this unlikely, but if so, why
should the third cycle start so bravely? The speeches of the
friends in the first two cycles do not vary greatly: Eliphaz, 47
and 34; Bildad, 21 and 20; Zophar 19 and 28. It is in the speeches
of Job that the differences in length are most marked: first cycle,
24 and 29; 21 and 34; 22 and 52; second cycle, 22 and 21,
16 and 22, 8 and 20; so-called third cycle, 13 and 16; 25 and 13,
? 22.

Chapters 25-27 introduce a whole mass of problems. The supposed dislocation of the speeches in a third cycle involves far
more than finding a whole speech for Zophar, another half-
speech for Bildad, and at the very least a half-speech from Job.
It involves all sorts of uncertainties within the chapters. Scholars
have sought to remedy what they have called 'the obvious confusion' of these chapters by reallocating the verses among Job
and the three friends. We need to remind ourselves again that
'obvious' means obvious on the basis of certain assumptions, and
that the more readily the word 'obvious' is used, the more it is
worthwhile questioning the assumptions. Here the initial assumption is that there was once a complete third cycle more or less on
the lines of the other two cycles. There is no evidence of this;
perhaps there never could be. Innumerable proposals have been
made, and rarely, if ever, do two scholars agree.[5] Indeed, some
passages are ascribed by one commentator or another to three of
the four speakers and to none of them.[6]

All claim that the confusion is in the book as it has come down
to us, but little attempt is made to account for such a wholesale

[4] If the usually accepted limits of the three cycles are accepted, then the
figures are 299, 186, 115; these make the situation still more difficult.

[5] See Appendix I for a summary of these proposed reconstructions. The
list is by no means complete, but it serves to indicate the very wide variation
of opinion.

[6] An example of what happens in these discussions is 27.7-23. Peake
ascribes this section to Bildad, but Marshall says it belongs to Job. Gray says
they belong to Zophar, while Lefèvre allocates them partly to Job and partly
to Zophar. Wellhausen, Kuenen and Dillmann do not ascribe them to anybody, but say they are a later insertion.

disturbance of the text. How could such a supposed confusion ever have been created except by a perversity of irresponsibility which is beyond all reasonable belief? Was it accidental? Perhaps the original material was on separate sheets and these were disturbed during transmission; perhaps the sheets were at some stage found loose and put into the wrong order.[7] But this kind of thing does not explain the supposed disarrangements in these chapters of the Book of Job, even though it might account for the entire loss of Zophar's speech. The dislocations vary far too much in length. Some are not nearly long enough, and others are far too long. Were the supposed changes deliberate? Such changes have been made, but in this case the purpose of the change should be clear. Compare, the alterations made in the writings of the Chronicler. In the Hebrew Bible, the story is that Ezra arrived in Jerusalem before Nehemiah, and that the final triumph was by Nehemiah, as related in Neh. 13. But in the LXX Esdras A (1 Esdras) there is a different order: II Chron. 35; 36; Ezra 1 4.7-24; the three children; Ezra 2.1-4.5; Ezra chs. 5-10. Neh. 7.73-78; 12. This story ends with the triumph by Ezra. According to one story Nehemiah was the successful founder of Judaism; according to the other Ezra was the founder.[8] Here the reasons for the deliberate changes are plain and clear. But this is not the case in the Book of Job. The result of the supposed changes is to create confusion.

The scholars are trying to force chs. 22-27 into a scheme into which they will not go. There never was any third cycle. Buhl was right when he said that these chapters consist of diverse fragments, but we do not think that they are of diverse authorship. They may well have been written by the poet who wrote the rest, but not properly fitted into the dialogue scheme. It looks as if the author began the fitting-in process, but did not complete it. He made an opening speech for Job (21.22-34), a speech for Eliphaz (ch. 22), and a reply by Job (ch. 23), but he got no farther. There is no scheme after the end of ch. 23. Fohrer has rightly recognized separate songs in ch. 24 and in 26.5-14, but we think he is unwise

[7] Compare, for instance, the order proposed for the Baal-tablets from Ugarit by G. R. Driver, *Canaanite Myths and Legends*, 1956, with the order in which the tablets were first arranged and are printed elsewhere.

[8] See N. H. Snaith, 'The Date of Ezra's Arrival in Jerusalem', *ZAW* 63 (1951) pp. 53-56; and Isaiah 40-66, A study of the teaching of the Second Isaiah and its Consequences', VTS, XIV (1967), pp. 250 f.

in seeking to construct a ninth speech for Job out of 26.1-4; 27.1-6, 11-12.

Another possible indication of the beginning of a fitting-in process is to be seen in the beginnings of what speeches there are. There are no preliminary couplets at the beginning of Eliphaz's speech in ch. 22; none at the beginning of Job's speech in ch. 23, and none at the beginning of Bildad's speech in ch. 25. The only instance of such an introduction hereabouts is 26.2f.

We are therefore of the opinion that in these chapters we have a collection of miscellaneous pieces, not placed in any recognizable order and not arranged according to any recognizable plan. These pieces extend from 24.1 to the end of ch. 28. Perhaps we ought to include in this miscellany the whole of 21.22-28.28.

It is quite possible for the prose introductions in chs. 22; 23; 25; 26; 37 to have been inserted by later scribes who were trying to be helpful. Particularly is this so for 27.1, which is similar to 29.1.[9]

Chapter 24 is a piece independent of the rest, just as ch. 28 is a separate piece. Fohrer is right here. It consists, just as ch. 28 does, of a series of answers to the question posed in the first couplet. In ch. 24 the couplet is: How does it come about that although the day of reckoning is known to God, yet those who know him do not know when it is? We do not understand this to refer to the final reckoning in the sense of the Last Judgment, the Day of the Great Assize. It deals with those occasions when the deeds of men meet with their just and proper reward in this present world. God has fixed the time when justice shall be done, the day when the wicked man shall be overthrown. But those who know him never know when this will be. Meanwhile every kind of wickedness flourishes. At first sight, this seems to be Job's problem all over again, but this is not so. At best, it is only a minor part of it. Job's problem all along has been that he has not been able to find justice anywhere, or ever, God allows the wicked to prosper and he does nothing at all to ease the troubles of the righteous or their poverty and distress. If the earth really does belong to God, then

[9] Compare the way in which the scribes of LXX have inserted in Codex Sin and sometimes in Codex A (but not in Codex B) notes in the Song of Songs, allocating verses to the bride, the bridegroom, and 'the daughters and the princesses and the friends of the bridegroom' (8.5), insertions which have had a major influence on the interpretation of the Song, not least in modern times.

he ought to do something about it. For the author, there never are any 'times'; that is his problem. Certainly the problem of the chapter is not the problem of the three friends. They indeed have no problem. Stubborn, established orthodoxy never has. The friends are completely sure that everything will be all right eventually for the righteous. They speak all the time as though they will see the downfall of the wicked rich and the vindication of the righteous poor man before he or they die. The problem of this chapter is different. The speaker does not deny that there is sudden disaster coming to the rich oppressor, and he believes, at least in theory, that there is prosperity coming for the righteous poor. But why is it that the poor man does not live to see it?

The most probable solution to the literary problems of chs. 24-28 is that in these chapters we have the further speculations of the author himself concerning the whole problem of God in his heaven and man on the earth, and that either he began to fit these ideas into his scheme but died before he proceeded very far, or found them too difficult, if not impossible, to fit into the scheme, and gave up. The ideas do not indeed fit easily, if at all, into those of Job or the three friends, and this is why the commentators have varied so much in their allocations of the verses in these chapters. The author may well have been just as uncertain as the commentators are as to whom these couplets should be allocated.

For many years scholars have recognized an independent piece in ch. 28, the so-called Poem on Wisdom. We do not think that ch. 28 or ch. 24 or any of the pieces in chs. 25-27 are interpolations in the sense that somebody else interpolated them. We ascribe them to the author himself, retained within the corpus of his writings.

VII

THE WISDOM POEM: CHAPTER 28

THE longest of all the pieces found hereabouts in the Book of Job, longer by three verses than ch. 24, is ch. 28; that is, if this chapter is indeed all of one piece. Recent scholars, almost without exception, regard the chapter as independent of the main structure of the book. By this they mean that it does not belong to the dialogue between Job and the three friends, and is also independent both of Job's soliloquy (3;29-31) and the Yahweh speeches. Many go still further and regard ch. 28 as being wholly independent even of the author of the dialogue.

There have been scholars,[1] mostly of earlier date, who have included ch. 28 in a reconstructed third cycle: Kennicott (Job's reply to Zophar), Hoffmann (Zophar's third speech), Bickell (before ch. 27 and part of Job's reply to Bildad), Lave (Zophar's third speech, followed by ch. 12 to provide a reply by Job).

But there are those who regard the chapter as being outside the main dialogue and yet by the same author. Dhorme regards the chapter as by the same author and thinks that it was deliberately placed between the speeches and the soliloquy. The editors of the Jerusalem Bible,[2] having tentatively placed 24.18-24 immediately before ch. 28, say that the thesis of ch. 28 is 'a preparation for that of the speech of Yahweh' and 'this literary personification (i.e. of wisdom) paves the way for the theology of the Word'. Terrien finds affinities in language and style with the Yahweh speeches, and he thinks that these may well be by the same author. It is true that in ch. 28 we find nothing directly applicable to the situation of Job, but that is true of a very great deal in chs. 24-27, indeed of almost everything in these chapters except perhaps 27.2-6 (7). R. H. Pfeiffer is inclined to think that ch. 28 'is an independent composition of the author, which is not an integral part of the poem', i.e. of the whole book. Budde and

[1] See Appendix I.
[2] See notes on p. 759.

64

Koenig, on the other hand, find a logical connection between this chapter and other parts of the book hereabouts. For Dhorme 'the author may very well be the same as he who wrote the poetic debate', and he bases this judgment on details of style and atmosphere, and on the part the chapter plays in the demonstration of man's inability compared with God's supreme knowledge and efficiency.

To us, ch. 28 is one of a number of pieces, all authentic: that is, all by the author of the rest of the book. These pieces have been placed between the two completed cycles of speeches (chs. 4-21 or 22) and chs. 29-31, the three chapters which, together with ch. 3, form Job's soliloquy.

But is ch. 28 itself a unity?

The Septuagint did not contain vv. 14-19, and they are supplied from Theodotion. This omission makes v. 20 follow close on v. 12 with only one couplet intervening. It is very unlikely that the poet would repeat at such a short interval a couplet which is to some degree a refrain: 'But where shall wisdom be found? And where is the home of understanding?' It is true that the omission of vv. 15-20 (Bickell, Dillmann, Budde) brings v. 14 with its reference to the deep sea and the sea into juxtaposition with the references to Abaddon and death in v. 22, and v. 22 is not impressive in the text as it stands. Verses 12-14 go together, and vv. 20-22 go together. We have three sections in the chapter. Vv. 1-11 are a picture of the miner searching underground for precious stones, and finding everything except wisdom-understanding, the one thing that is truly worth finding. Verses 12-19 say that wisdom-understanding can never be found by man nor bought. The great underworld knows nothing of it. Money and jewels will buy everything except wisdom-understanding, the one thing that is worth buying. Verses 20-28 say that God knows where it is to be found. He sees everything and everywhere. If any man wishes to know what this wisdom involves for man, this wisdom which no man can ever find and no man can every buy, then he has two excellent working rules. One is 'the fear of the Lord'. The other is 'depart from evil'.

Duhm's solution is to tidy up the poem and make all the verses march in regular, rhythmical order as if on military parade. He assumed that the chapter originally began with the couplet of

---

[3] *Job*, ET, pp. li, xcvii.

vv. 12 and 20: 'And wisdom, where is it to be found? And where
is the home of understanding?' This certainly tidies up the poem
considerably, and it provides three stanzas, vv. 1-11, 12-19, 20-28
(29). But Duhm goes still further, and he inserts this same couplet
in between vv. 6 and 7. This creates one stanza dealing with
underground workings, and a second stanza (8-11) dealing with
birds and predatory animals. What Gunkel did by way of regi-
menting the text of the Psalms and what Wickes did for regi-
menting the accents of the Poetical Books, Duhm does for ch. 28
of the Book of Job. But Duhm's scheme halts at v. 9, where
we are back again with the miner. This led Peake to think
of vv. 7-8 as being misplaced, and he would insert them after
v. 12. Budde thought of vv. 5-6 as a later addition, and he also
omitted v. 24 on the ground that it suggests that perhaps
wisdom after all has a home on the earth. Duhm does not like
this verse either, and he transfers it to follow v. 11. But all that
v. 24 says is that God can look everywhere, and can see right
to the ends of the earth beneath the overhanging sky. It is
difficult to see how this can mean that God thinks wisdom may
have a home on earth. Rather, it appears to mean that God
knows very well that it has no such home, because he can
look everywhere and see everything, and if there had been such
a home on earth, he most certainly would have seen it. We see
no reason, therefore, to suppose that v. 24 is in the wrong place.

Here again, so many different solutions have been proposed,
it seems likely that what is at fault is not the poem, but the
attitude of mind which would make the poem into a regiment on
parade, with equal companies and precise ranks. The ancients did
not work in that hyper-precise pattern. It is a demand for precision
which exists only in the not-so-modern west. Who ever saw a
picture hung straight in India?

We turn to v. 28. Some commentators have argued against the
inclusion of this verse in the original poem. They say that the
wisdom of the previous verse is virtually personified, and that
wisdom belongs to the realm of the divine. They say that in v. 28
we are dealing with practical wisdom, with the way in which a
man ought to live his life day by day, with that practical wisdom
which is the proper way of living in this world of men and things.
All this is perfectly right, but in our view it confirms the genuine-
ness of the verse.

The conclusion that what is said in our last paragraph militates against the inclusion of the last verse of the chapter in the original poem is faulty on two grounds.

First: It forgets that the poem is concerned from first to last with man's search for that wisdom which will enable him to live properly and happily on earth for his allotted span. He seeks it as the miner seeks ore and precious stones in tunnels that slant down beneath the surface of the earth. He asks the great birds of prey, those huge birds with the proverbial wing-span, which hover high in the sky and can cover with their sight huge areas of land. He turns to the wild beasts who wander freely where they will. Wisdom is not in the heavens; it is nowhere to be seen under the canopy of the sky. Nor is it buried in the earth. It is not in the great ocean deep of the primeval sea that is round and beneath the world. It is not below that, in Sheol, the abode of the dead, neither is it below even Sheol in the Abaddon which lies under all. Not all the treasures of earth can buy it. God alone knows where it is to be found. This is because it is his and his alone. It belongs to the High God, far removed and for ever remote from man. This is why no mortal man can ever find it and never can share it. Thus wisdom, its nature and origin, becomes part of the problem of the whole book, part of the problem of the High God who is so far removed from mortal man that for all practical purposes he might never exist at all. But—and this is the whole point of ch. 28—this High God has given man a practical working rule, one which he can follow and can apply. For God and for God alone, there is wisdom, and it is this wisdom which is the basis and material of creation. By this wisdom God created the cosmos, and by this wisdom he maintains it in effectual working. Man cannot have *this* wisdom, but there is a wisdom for men. This human wisdom consists of the working rule of v. 28. Fear God and shun moral evil. Here is the basis of that practical wisdom which is a characteristic of the thought of the later wise men of Israel. It is further developed in parts of Proverbs and in some respects it reaches its peak in the Wisdom of Ben Sira (Ecclesiasticus). It is the foundation of the *halakah* of the scribes: those rules of the rabbis according to which a man must walk. This wisdom is 'our only wisdom here'.[4]

[4] See Charles Wesley's hymn (no. 576 in the Methodist Hymnbook of 1933):

Second: we deprecate the rigid line which some scholars adopt concerning the personification of wisdom, making the main question which is to be answered: Is wisdom personified or not? We find this to be a muddled question, and naturally it receives a muddled answer. It is similar to the question often asked in the study of primitive religion: Is *mana* personal or impersonal? This question cannot be answered, because it is a wrong question. The whole concept of *mana* belongs to a world of thought where our modern clear-cut distinction between personal and impersonal is very far indeed from being made. 'Mana' is an animist conception. When we speak of animism we are wrong to say that it involves personifying external objects, as though there was any choice between personifying and not personifying. There is no such choice for animists. This was the way they thought. Using our terms: they were not thinking personally and they were not thinking impersonally. They were thinking; and they had no other way of thinking. Animism consists of thinking in this parti-cular way, where *all* things are living things. They did not make the distinction between personal and impersonal. It is probable they did not even make a distinction between living and not living. All things were alive. Something of the same kind of thing is to be found in Hebrew thought. The very phrase 'virtual per-sonification', which is sometimes used of wisdom, shows that we are dealing with what we would call the borderland between personification and non-personification. Notice also the way in which in the Old Testament *rūaḥ* (spirit) is sometimes regarded as a 'stuff', so that Paul Volz can rightly use the word *Rūḥ-Stoff*[5] of this particular stage of thought.

To pass on: much has been made of the similarity of the couplet in v. 28 to Prov. 15.23; Ps. 111.10, together with Prov. 1.7 and 9.10. What similarity there is, is almost entirely confined to the first line of the couplet. There is no repetition even of one line. The phrase 'fear of the Lord' occurs in the first line of all five

> Be it my only wisdom here
> To serve the Lord with filial fear,
>   And loving gratitude;
> Superior sense may I display,
> By shunning every evil way,
>   And walking in the good.

[5] *Der Geist Gottes im Alten Testament und im ausschliessenden Judentum*, 1910, p. 27.

verses, three times in the first half of the line and twice in the second half. The word *ḥokmā* (wisdom) occurs in all five verses, but never twice in the same phrase. The similarity is far from being exact.

Job 28.28	*yr't 'dny hy' ḥkmh*
	wswr mr' bynh
Prov. 15.33	*yr't yhwh mwsr ḥkmh*
	wlpny kbwd 'nwh
Ps. 111.10	*r'šyt ḥkmh yr't yhwh*
	škl ṭwb lkl 'syhm
Prov. 9.10	*tḥlt ḥkmh yr't yhwh*
	wd't qdšym bynh
Prov. 1.7	*yr't yhwh r'šyt d't*
	ḥkmh wmswr 'wylym bzw

Job 28.28	The fear of the Lord, that is wisdom;
	And turning from evil is understanding.
Prov. 15.33	The fear of the Lord is instruction in wisdom;
	And before honour is humility.
Ps. 111.10	The beginning of Wisdom is the fear of the Lord;
	Good insight to all who do them.
Prov. 9.10	The start of wisdom is the fear of the Lord,
	And knowledge of the Holy One(s) is understanding.
Prov. 1.7	The fear of the Lord is the beginning of knowledge,
	Wisdom and correction fools despise.

For us, the whole point of the poem is in this last verse, and the prose introduction of this last verse appeals to us in a most emphatic way. It breaks off the verse plainly from the rest, and it allows the 'moral' of the poem to be expressed in a complete and deliberate couplet. When the poem says that wisdom belongs to the High God alone and is completely and for ever unattainable by man, it is wholly in accordance with the general tenor of the author's sentiments as expressed in the speeches of Job. The whole problem revolves round the conception of the High God. If wisdom belongs to him alone, what can mortal man do? The answer fundamentally is: nothing at all. But there is a practical suggestion, and it is contained in the concluding verse. For man on earth it means: Fear God and turn away from evil. This is the sound, practical basis of a religion based on the speculations of the wise, of all those who by the process of thought seek to discover the proper way in which a man is to live in this world.

It has been maintained that the wisdom of v. 28 is different from the wisdom of the rest of the chapter. Of course it is. There are two 'wisdoms' in the Old Testament. One is the wisdom which belongs to God alone, and was the instrument or the companion of the High God in his work of creation. The other is that practical human wisdom, that informed common sense coupled with shrewdness which enables a man to live and prosper in this created world. The situation is analogous to, though entirely independent of, the Greek idea of the Logos, to the extent that there are, so to speak, two: the Creative word and the logos (reason, speech, word) in man. It is wrong to say that in v. 28 the wisdom of the previous verses is revealed to mortal man. (Certainly it is wrong to say 'discovered by'.) This is not so, and it can never be so. Mortal man can never discover nor apprehend the divine wisdom, the heavenly wisdom, but he can have a practical substitute for it. It is this practical application of the heavenly wisdom to human affairs which prevents the Hebrew wisdom (*ḥokmā*) from being as solely speculative and intellectual as the Greek wisdom (*sophia*). To whatever degree at any time Hebrew wisdom may have become speculative and intellectual (e.g. when Maimonides sought to do for Judaism what Thomas Aquinas did for Christianity, both with Aristotle as the master of them that know), Hebrew wisdom was always essentially functional and practical. This is as true of heavenly wisdom as of earthly wisdom. It must always be 'efficient in working'. If a man cannot know wisdom as God knows it, then there must be a wisdom which he can know and understand. Verse 28 indicates what this earthly wisdom is. This verse is the nearest the author ever gets to a solution of his problem.

There is also an objection to this verse because of its so-called lack of balance. Such comments are largely subjective. But the Syriac version and one Kennicott MS (no. 76) omit the initial *hēn* (behold), though in any case this interjection could be regarded as being outside the metrical structure of the verse. The rest of the verse could then well pass as a good couplet with 'wisdom' balancing 'understanding', and 'fear of the Lord' balancing 'turning from evil', and the couplet all the more impressive as a concluding couplet because of its deliberate 2 plus 2: 3 structure.[6]

A third objection is the unique (in this book) occurrence of

Compare the way in which English poets have used an Alexandrine line

'ᵃ*dōnāy* as the name of God. But if the tetragrammaton itself had
been found here, that also would have been said to be remarkable,
since the form YHWH is found once only in the verse portions
of the Book (12.9), apart from the introductions to the Yahweh
speeches. But even in 12.9 there are seven MSS in de Rossi's list
which have 'ᵉ*lōah*. It is dangerous to build much on the use of a
divine name in any particular instance, apart from the general use
of the name YHWH in the Yahwist tradition and of 'ᵉ*lōhīm* in the
Elohist tradition, both in the Pentateuch and in the Psalms.
Further in Job 28.28, one hundred MSS read YHWH, four read
'ᵃ*dōnāy* YHWH and two omit it altogether. The fact that in the
Hebrew text generally in a particular instance some MSS have
YHWH and some have 'ᵃ*dōnāy* does not in itself mean a great
deal, since some have the one against their own masora, and some
the other against their masora. What really matters in these cases
is the authority behind the manuscript and the opinion of the
reader as to what constitutes the best Masoretic authority,
whether Ben Asher (Maimonides), Ben Naphtali (Rabbi Saadiya),
or whether we ought to accept the full development of Masoretic
traditions in Baer and Delitzsch. Further, the occurrence of the
two names YHWH 'ᵃ*dōnāy* almost invariably means that the
copyist wrote the sacred name and then realized that he ought to
have written the substitute, but being a pious Jewish scribe he
could not scratch out the tetragrammaton, so he left it and added
the other. Sometimes the scribe realized his mistake before he
finished the word. This accounts for such curious forms as
y'dny, yh'dny and *yhw'dny*. There can be no doubt that the correct
text in Job 28.28 is 'ᵃ*dōnāy*.

---

of six feet to end a song written with five feet to the line. Critics who object
to such a procedure are like Alexander Pope:

A needless Alexandrine ends the song,
That like a wounded snake drags its slow length along.

a couplet which in itself is an admirable example of the effect of an
Alexandrine.

VIII

THE SPEECHES OF ELIHU: CHAPTERS 32-37

THERE are two main questions concerning these six chapters: Are they by the author of the rest of the book? Were they interpolated into the rest of the book? If the answer to the first question is 'No', then the answer to the second question must be 'Yes'. If the answer to the first question is 'Yes', then the answer to the second question may be either 'No' or 'Yes'.

The speeches of Elihu come immediately after the note 'The words of Job are ended' (31.40), and immediately before the Yahweh speeches. The majority of Old Testament scholars regard these Elihu speeches as a later addition, and as an insertion by a later author. Usually they treat both problems (unity of authorship and interpolation) as one. The idea that the speeches are not part of the original book, as it left the author's hands, goes back as far as Eichhorn (1803). But Budde went so far as to maintain that these chapters are the most important chapters in the book, since in them the author offers his own solution.[1] Substantially the same position, at least so far as authorship is concerned, has been maintained by C. H. Cornill.[2] A list of recent advocates of this view is given by H. H. Rowley.[3]

Our view is that these Elihu speeches are by the author of the

[1] This view is found both in his *Beiträge zur Kritik des Buches Hiob*, 1876, pp. 65ff. and in his *Das Buch Hiob*, 2nd ed., 1913, pp. xxivff. See also Posselt, *Der Verfasser der Elihu Reden*, 1909.

[2] *Einleitung in das Alte Testament*, ET, *Introduction to the Canonical Books of the Old Testament*, 1907.

[3] 'The Meaning of Job', *Bulletin of the John Rylands Library*, 41 (1958), p. 175. It includes W. S. Bruce (1928), Kallen (1928), Dennefeld (1935), Szczygield (1931), Eerdmans (1939), Kroeze (1943), Dubarle (1946). Steinmüller (1944), Humbert (1955). Others who think that the speeches are authentic are Rosenmüller (1924), Umbreit (1932), Stickel (1842), Wildeboer (1895), Thilo (1925). Recently there has been A. Guillaume, 'The Unity of the Book of Job', *The Annual of the Leeds University Oriental Society*, IV (1964) pp. 26-46, being part of his thesis that the book was written in Arabia and that there are very many Arabisms in the book. See also, but based in literary considerations, R. Gordis, 'Elihu the Intruder', *Biblical and Other Studies*, ed. A. Altmann, 1963, pp. 60-78, and *The Book of God and Man*, 1965.

rest of the book. We do not think that they were in his first draft, which consisted[4] of the prologue and the epilogue (without 2.11-13 and 42.7-9 and the phrase 'when he prayed for his friend', 42.10), Job's soliloquy (3; 29-31) and the Yahweh speeches (38-41). Further, we do not think that the Elihu speeches came into the book at the same time as the dialogue between the three friends and Job, but we do think that they are the creation of the original author of the Hebrew Job and that they are as character- istic of him as any of the rest. It may be that Budde was right when he said that it is in these Elihu speeches that the key to the intention of the author is to be found, but we do not think so. In our view, he had three different intentions at three different times.[5]

The Arguments against the Authenticity of the Elihu Speeches

1. It is pointed out that Elihu is not mentioned in either the prologue or the epilogue; in fact, he is not mentioned anywhere except in the seven chapters themselves. Also the whole of the seven chapters could be cut out and, judging from the rest of the book, nobody would ever know that they had ever been there.

This certainly is so. But if we omit the last three verses of the prologue and the first three verses of the epilogue plus the curious phrase in 42.10, we can say the same of the three friends. There is nothing in chapters 3; 29-31 and nothing in the Yahweh speeches which would lead us to suppose that the three friends ever existed. Indeed, the account in the epilogue of the way in which Job's friends and relations clustered round and how they each gave him a present is not easy, as we have seen, to fit in with the three friends and their speeches. It is very much more in keeping with the old folk-lore style of the prose story of Job. Any argument on these lines advanced in favour of the exclusion of Elihu from the author's work applies also to the three friends.

In any case, even supposing that Elihu came into the Book of Job at the same time as the three friends, we see no absolute necessity for introducing him in 2.11-13 at the same time as the three friends are introduced. That would spoil the effect both of their entry and of his. The author has a much better sense of drama than to destroy the effect of either entry. It is natural that there should be no reference to Elihu until he actually intervenes,

---

[4] See above, pp. 34-44.   [5] See above, pp. 10, 92ff.

and it is natural also that Elihu should refer directly and explicitly to what both Job and the three friends have said. It is indeed 'obvious that the rest of the book has been written without any knowledge of these speeches'.[6] We agree also that 'they form no part of the original work', but this does not necessarily mean that they are by another author. Further, what reference to the Elihu speeches could there possibly be in the dialogue? And also, if the absence of any reference to Elihu in the Yahweh speeches is to be regarded as decisive, what about the three friends? They might never have existed so far as any reference to them is concerned in chs. 37-39 and 40-41.

The omission of Elihu from the epilogue is more significant. It is difficult to see how there could be no reference to him if he had been in the book when the epilogue attained its present form. We conclude that Elihu came into the book later.

2. A second argument against the authenticity of the Elihu speeches is that they are superfluous and so add nothing substantial to what the three friends have had to say. It is also said that the Elihu speeches anticipate much of what is said in the Yahweh speeches. Still further, it is maintained that Elihu fails to meet Job's case equally with the three friends. If it is assumed that Elihu is seeking to deal with the problem of suffering and especially of the suffering of the righteous, then it is true that he makes virtually no progress. Further, it is also true that he says some things which are also found in the Yahweh speeches. But our view is that Elihu is not particularly concerned with the problem of suffering as such. He is the young man out against the old orthodoxy, and this is why he feels free to criticize Job as well as the three friends. For Job is orthodox, though puzzled. This attack on orthodoxy is a new element in the Elihu speeches. Job may make offensive remarks about the aged and the wise, but he still is orthodox. As to the charge that Elihu does not meet Job's case, what solution can anybody propose for this problem of the relation between the High-God and this world of men and things? There are two possible answers. One is that of the Book of Job—submission. The other[7] is a true Incarnation and its demonstration of the everlasting mercy. But that is, indeed, another story; it is the Christian story.

[6] Driver-Gray, Job, p. xl.
[7] As indicated by Egdar Jones, *The Triumph of Job*, 1966, p. 118.

3. The third objection is concerned with the differences in style. Scholars have claimed to be able to detect differences in style between the speeches of Elihu and the rest of the book. It is alleged that Elihu is tautologous, that he is a wind-bag, a cocksure young man, and so forth. Doubtless all this is what the three friends thought. It is what age in every generation tends to think of ebullient, reforming youth. But Budde[8] argued for similarity of style, and so did Posselt.[9] A. Guillaume[10] also argues for a common vocabulary. Budde and Posselt proved their case to the extent that Driver-Gray say[11]: 'In spite of very much that is common.' They explain this as being 'the natural result of the familiarity of the writer with the book he was supplementing'. It is evident that there is a certain similarity of style. But what differences in style can be detected in the various parts of the book?

The alleged differences of style comprise five aspects: (*a*) the use of the prepositions, (*b*) the use of divine names, (*c*) the use of the two first person singular personal pronouns, (*d*) the so-called Aramaisms, (*e*) the use of rare words.

(*a*) The use of prepositions

Driver-Gray[12] give an analysis of the rarer (? archaic) forms of prepositions in the Book of Job, and they give comparative figures. They say: 'No doubt several of these forms occur too infrequently to have much or any significance. But the significance of the whole group is hardly to be cancelled by the considerations which Budde and Posselt have brought forward.'[13] It certainly is the case that almost all of these unusual forms of prepositions are found more often in the Book of Job than anywhere else in the Old Testament.[14] If the length of the poetic portions of the Book of Job is considered in comparison with the length of the rest of the Old Testament, or even against the rest of the poetry in the Old Testament, then the greater frequency of these particular forms is most marked. But what is still more important is to notice the

[8] *Beiträge zur Kritik des Buches Hiob*, pp. 92-113.
[9] *Der Verfasser der Elihureden*, pp. 67-111.
[10] *The Annual of the Leeds University Oriental Society*, IV, pp. 26-46.
[11] *Job*, p. xii.   [12] *ibid.*, p. xiv.   [13] *ibid.*, p. xlvi.
[14] The figures are: *ᵃlē* 15 times in Job as against 25 elsewhere; *ᵃdē*, 2 against 10; *ᵉlē*, 4 against 0; *bᵉmō*, 4 against 4; *kᵉmō*, 11 against 32; *lᵉmō*, 4 against 0; *minni*, 19 against 13; *bᵉli* (without prefix), 10 against 11; *lāmō*, 10 against 45; *ᵃlēmō*, 8 against 4.

kind of forms they are. All these uncommon forms are archaic forms, and they look like archaic forms deliberately retained and used. This gives us a clue to the author's general style, and it is a very important clue. His style is essentially literary, and it is the only piece of sustained literary writing in the Old Testament. Parts of Proverbs are literary and deliberately so, but not for so nearly so sustained a stretch of time. Occasional psalms are consciously literary. The Song of Songs is our only ancient surviving Hebrew lyric. Other books of the Old Testament are primarily historical, usually reproducing more or less *verbatim* older traditions. Or the books are legal or prophetic or liturgical. But this book is primarily literary. The author uses deliberately archaic forms. His is a sophisticated, a super-elegant style. This mostly is what has made the book so difficult to translate, and all ages have found it so. He often uses words with their archaic meaning.[15] This is true of the whole book, not of the Elihu speeches only. Further, if the critics are right in finding more of these archaic prepositions and words in the Elihu speeches, then it means that the poet's style has developed more and more along these lines. He is being more successful in producing his own special style, even to the point where style and precise and elegant parallelisms tend to overwhelm the rest. We do not think, however, that the figures warrant the assumption that there are enough additional archaic prepositions in the Elihu speeches to justify any significant judgment.[16] In so far as any increase may be discerned in the Elihu speeches, we would say that this is the true explanation of what the critics call verbose and tautologous: it is actually an over-development of literary elegance.[17]

[15] See Appendix II.

[16] The figures are: $^a l\bar{e}$, 2 in the Elihu speeches against 13 elsewhere in Job; $^o d\bar{e}$, 0 against 2; $^e l\bar{e}$, 0 against 4; $b^e m\bar{o}$, 1 against 3(4); $k^e m\bar{o}$, 0(1) against 11; $l^e m\bar{o}$, 0(1) against 4; *minni*, 3 against 16; $b^e l\bar{\iota}$, 2 against 8; $l\bar{a}m\bar{o}$, 0 against 10; $^a l\bar{e}m\bar{o}$, 0 against 8. There are six chapters of Elihu speeches as against thirty-three other verse-chapters. Our estimate is that the proportions are as nearly equal as any reasonable person could expect.

[17] The figures can be studied in another way. To give the number of these archaic forms is not enough; we need also to give the number of the ordinary forms of the prepositions. The figures for the archaic $^a l\bar{e}$ are 2 in Elihu and 13 elsewhere in the book; for the usual form $'al$, the figures are 15 and 61. The figures for the archaic $^a d\bar{e}$ are 0 and 2; for the usual $'ad$ they are 2 and 21. The figures for the archaic $^e l\bar{e}$ are 0 and 4; for the usual $'el$ they are 6 and 26. According to the number of verses in the two sets of passages, the proportions should be 1 to 5 or 6. The figures for distribution are so near to the normal expected that they lead to no conclusion as to separate authorship.

No. of Chapters	Section	ʿolē	ʿal	ʿadē	ʿad	ʾelē	ʾel	bᵉmō	kᵉmō	lᵉmō	minnī	belī	lᵃmō	ʿalēmō
6	Elihu: 32-37	2	15	0	2	0	6	1	10	?1	3	2	0	0
4	Job: 3, 29-31	4	6	0	1	2	1	0	1	1	2	2	2	3
11	1st cycle: 4-14	3	21	1	11	1	12	?1	5	0	7	1	2	1
7	2nd cycle: 15-21	4	17	1	2	1	6	3	1	0	6	0	1	2
7	Miscellaneous: 22-28	0	10	0	4	0	1	0	1	1	1	1	4	2
2	Yahweh: 38-39	1	6	0	3	0	3	0	1	1	0	2	1	0
—	Job: 40.1-5	0	0	0	0	0	0	0	0	1	0	0	0	0
2	Yahweh: 40-41	1	1	0	0	0	3	0	2	0	0	1	0	0

We have divided the chapters into cycles according to the usual custom, since the tables in Driver-Gray are drawn up in this way. If we adopt the allocation of chapters to cycles which we have advocated (see above, pp. 9f.), the results are virtually the same.

We have drawn up a list of the numbers of the occurrences of these archaic forms and their more normal equivalents in the various parts of the book, and our assessment of the figures is that nothing can be proved from them to show that more than one author has been at work. The proportions are roughly the same. The only possible deduction, so far as we can see, is that, if the argument is of any value, there is a difference observable between the miscellaneous chs. 22-28 and the rest.

(b) The use of the various names of God

Driver-Gray[18] give a table of the relative frequency of the three names '*ēl*, '*elōah* and *šadday*. Their conclusion is: 'Elihu shows a marked preference for '*ēl*, using this name more frequently than all the other Names of God put together, whereas in the Dialogue '*elōah* is used with the same frequency, and *šadday* also frequently.' This statement is based on a simple count, but we do not think this is a proper approach to the problem of distribution. If all the chapters were in prose, this approach would be right and proper. But these chapters are not in prose. They are in verse, almost wholly in 3:3 couplets, and to a great extent in quite sophisticated and precise couplets. Nowhere in the Old Testament are the couplets more elegant than here, and nowhere does there appear to be so much care exercised. Indeed, if regard is paid to the author's fondness for the archaic meaning of words, the exact parallelism is much more pronounced than is normally realized. By this we mean that, time and again, the recognition that such and such a word is used with its archaic meaning has established an exact parallelism which previously has gone unrecognized. It is essential, therefore, that we examine the frequency of the three names as (1) first choice and (2) second choice. Which name did the poet put down first in a couplet? Having made his first choice and thereby limited his second choice, what name did he select to put into the second half of his couplet? It is not easy to imagine two questions which more surely expose the unconscious preference of the writer. Driver-Gray[19] mention this aspect of the author's choice, but they do not give it sufficient prominence as against their figures which give the actual number of occurrences. The poet's choice for the first half of the couplet is virtually un-

[18] *Job*, p. xliii.
[19] *ibid.*, p. xliii.

fettered, and his choice for the second half of the couplet is
necessarily restricted. This is the table:

No. of Chapters	Section	'ēl		'elōah		šadday	
		1st	2nd	1st	2nd	1st	2nd
6	Elihu: 32-37	19	0	6	0	2	4
4	Job: 3; 29-31	3	0	5	0	2	1
11	1st Cycle: 4-14	8	1	11	?2	3	4
7	2nd cycle: 15-21	10	1	9	0	3	1
7	Miscellaneous: 22-28	9	0	3	2	5	5
2	Yahweh: 38-39	1	0	1	0	0	0
—	Job: 40.1-5	0	0	0	1	1	0
2	Yahweh: 40-41	2	0	0	0	0	0

Thus, 'ēl is the first choice in the Elihu speeches 19 times as
against 33 times in the rest of the book, and the second choice 0
against 2; 'elōah is first choice 6 times as against 29, and second
choice 0 against 5; šadday is first choice 2 against 14, and second
choice 4 against 11. We have neglected the occurrences of
'elōhīm, since they are few; 2 in the Elihu speeches (32.2; 34.9),
the first of which is in the prose introduction; 1 in 28.23; and 2
(5.8; 20.29) as a parallel to 'ēl. (38.7 is not a name of God.)[20]

Why does the poet have a preference for the two names, 'ēl
and 'elōah?

The name 'ēl is used because this is the name of the High God
throughout the whole area. It has been the name of the High God
in Syria from time immemorial, and this is confirmed in the
Ugarit tablets. This is why the Hebrews adopted it as a parallel
name for Yahweh. They equated Yahweh with El, the High God
of Canaan.[21] The whole discussion in the Book of Job ranges

[20] Further details: 'ēl and 'elōah are found once only in the same couplet
(12.6), 'ēl and 'elōhīm are found as parallels twice only, 'ēl first in 5.8 and
'elōhīm first in 20.29. It seems to be the case that 'ēl and 'elōhīm are not regarded
as fit companions in a couplet, probably because they are too similar in
sound. The first choice throughout is 'ēl or 'elōah, and the occurrences are
on the whole equally divided, though both in the Elihu speeches and in the
miscellenous chs. 22-28 the proportion is three to one in favour of 'ēl. This
is the only difference in distribution we have been able to detect in the use of
the three names. The name šadday is scarcely ever used in the first half of a
couplet unless it is the only divine name in the couplet, but it is the usual
name throughout in the second line when there are two names used in the
couplet.

[21] See N. H. Snaith, 'The Advent of Monotheism in Israel', *The Annual of
the Leeds University Oriental Society*, V (1965), pp. 100-13, where it is argued

around the apparent non-activity and isolation of this High God. Does the High God care about justice in this world? or about anything else, for that matter? Why is it that apparently he does so very little to ensure justice in the affairs of men? Is it really true that he is so remote and so terrible that he does not hear prayer and entreaty? These considerations are fully adequate for the choice of the name *'ēl*. One of the features of primitive religion is the remoteness of the High God. Often he is not worshipped at all. Sometimes he is altogether otiose. Worship is offered to the nearer gods, the low gods, the gods who control the weather, the rain and consequently the fertility. This is why there are so few obvious traces of the High God among some primitive peoples that those investigators who accept the Frazer-Tylor theories of development up through animatism, animism, ancestor-worship, monolatry with an ultimate monotheism, find no trace of him. They do not ask the right questions, and do not realize that wherever there are low gods, there is always a High God also, always remote, usually shadowy and sometimes virtually forgotten—in any case too dreadful ever to name.[22]

The name *'ᵉlōah* is archaic, so that the choice of this name is partly due to the dominant idea of the High God, but partly also to the author's general archaic style. We have noticed this culti-vated archaic literary style in connection with the use of pre-positions.[23] It has been argued that this word *'ᵉlōah* is a singular formed late by inference as a back-formation from the plural form *'ᵉlōhīm*, and this may indeed be so. On the other hand, it may well be an ancient name for the High God.[24]

The name for the second choice is usually *šadday* throughout the book. The Elihu speeches show no variation here. Indeed, the use of any other name as a second choice is rare throughout the

that the Hebrews identified Yahweh with El and not with Baal, so that the tendency was to worship Yahweh-El and Baal.

[22] *Ibid.*   [23] See above, pp. 75-78.

[24] Cf. Arabic *'ilāhat*, and also in Samaritan, Aramaic, Syriac, Sabaean. The form is used four (five) times of any god, a heathen (idol) god: II Kings 17.31 (Kethib only); Hab. 1.11; Dan. 11.37, II Chron. 32.15; Job 12.6; of which two are probably late. But mostly it is the name of the God of Israel. It is used three times in ancient poems, Deut. 32.15, 17 and Ps. 18.32 (EVV 31). For the rest, it is used 42 times in Job and 7 times elsewhere, Isa. 44.8; Hab. 3.3 (probably a very ancient poem); Prov. 30.5; Pss. 50.22; 114.7; 139.19 and especially Neh. 9.19, where Ex. 34.6 is quoted but with *'ᵉlōah* instead of *'ēl*. The name *'ᵉlōah* is therefore chosen certainly because it has an archaic flavour, and probably also because it is a genuine name of the High God.

book. This name is an archaism. It is used in ancient poems: in Num. 24.4 and 16, deliberately as an archaism in Ruth 1.20 and 21; and five times elsewhere including another deliberate archaism in Ps. 91.1. But it is used thirty-one (thirty-two) times in Job. The combination '*ēl šadday* is not found in Job, but eight times elsewhere, including the ancient poem, Gen. 49.25.

We have thus gained nothing in our investigation of the uses of the various names of God to indicate any diverse authorship in the Book of Job. What we have gained is an increased understanding of the author's problem concerning the apparent non-activity of the High God, and a strong conviction concerning the literary style of the author. He has an archaic style and he shows every indication of seeking deliberately to cultivate it. This man loves archaic forms and archaic words.[25]

(*c*) *The use of* '*aní* *and* '*ānōkī, the two forms of the first person singular pronoun*

Driver-Gray[26] produced figures which they thought supported the statement that in the Elihu speeches there is a definite preference for '*aní*. Here is a list which has been drawn up on the same lines as the previous lists:

No of Chapters	Section	'*aní*		'*ānōkī*	
		1st choice	2nd choice	1st choice	2nd choice
6	Elihu: 32-37	9	0	1	2
4	Job: 3; 29-31	1	0	5	1
11	1st cycle: 4-14	10	0	1	0
7	2nd cycle: 2-21	3	0	0	0
7	Miscellaneous: 22-28	0	0	0	0
2	Yahweh 38-39	0	0	0	0
—	Job: 40.1-5	0	0	0	0
2	Yahweh: 40-41	1	0	0	0
1	Epilogue	0	—	1	—
2	Prologue	4	—	0	—

The occurrence of '*ānōkī* in 12.3 is doubtful (? repetition of 13.2), and 21.4 is doubtful also (not in Syriac). Probably also the '*aní* in 9.21 ought not to be counted. The use of these two personal pronouns does not vary from section to section, except in Job's

[25] See also E. Dhorme, *Job*, pp. lxv-lxxii.
[26] *Job*, p. xliii.

soliloquy (chs. 3; 29-31) where the variation is marked. These are the chapters which we believe to belong to the author's first draft, the Hebrew Job which is comparable to the Babylonian Job. The author prefers '*ᵃnī* throughout, except in his earliest work. The pronoun '*ᵃnī* is used twice in the same couplet on two occasions, 32.17 and 33.6, and each time it is for emphasis. Also, the use of *'ānōkī* at the beginning of 29.16 follows an '*ᵃnī* at the end of the previous verse, so this is virtually a second choice rather than a first choice.

Our conclusion from this examination of the use of the two pronouns is that the author initially preferred *'ānōkī*, but that later, when the three friends and Elihu were introduced into the work, he preferred '*ᵃnī*. The fact that the first person is used with greater frequency in the Elihu speeches is explained by the nature of the speeches themselves. Elihu is saying what he himself thinks in contrast to what the others have said.

(d) The so-called Aramaisms

It is claimed that the number of Aramaisms in the Elihu speeches is proportionately greater than in the rest of the book, and that they constitute so marked a feature of the style as to confirm the idea that these chapters are of different authorship. As Driver-Gray say[27] this feature has been exaggerated by some, and also (they say) minimized by others.[28]

What exactly constitutes an Aramaism? Guillaume maintained that there are none at all in the Elihu speeches and only one doubtful example in the rest of the book.[29] This is part of his theory that the book was written in Arabia, and he aims to show that there are many Arabisms in the book, especially from the Hijaz. It may well be that Guillaume allowed himself less stringent

[27] *Job*, p. xlvi.

[28] It was estimated by Kautzsch that there are 32 Aramaisms in the whole book. Of these, 5 are common to the Elihu speeches and the rest of the book; 8 are peculiar to Elihu; 19 are peculiar to the rest of the book. Of those that are peculiar to the two sections (Elihu, 8; the rest 19), the proportion is 1 to 2.4. For total numbers in each section (13 and 24), the proportion is 1 to 1.8. The number of chapters is 6 and 33, a proportion of 1 to 5.5. Thus, assuming that all these are indeed Aramaisms, there are proportionately more of them in the Elihu speeches than elsewhere. How significant this difference is, is a matter at least partly of subjective judgment. But for the most part it depends upon what exactly these so-called Aramaisms are held to be.

[29] *The Annual of the Leeds University Oriental Society*, IV (1964), p. 27.

tests than most in deciding what roots are common to Hebrew and Arabic, but some of his equations are certainly sound. Considering the small amount of Hebrew literature which has survived from pre-Christian times, considering also the very much smaller amount we have of truly literary compositions, we maintain that if a word conforms to the rules which govern the changes of consonant between language and language and if a comparable meaning can be found elsewhere than in Aramaic (say, in Arabic, Ugarit, Accadian, Ethiopic), then the word is not an Aramaism. It is a comparatively rare word, one with which a 'literary' writer and a learned man is more likely to be familiar than a man who was primarily a prophet. After all, the men responsible for the wisdom literature of Israel were learned men. They may very well be presumed to have had a much larger vocabulary than others, especially since they were familiar with literature other than Hebrew literature. There is no room for doubt here; they were familiar with the wisdom literature of other peoples of the Fertile Crescent.

It is necessary for these so-called Aramaisms to be discussed in detail, since for many scholars they loom large in the discussions. This involves detailed linguistic examination, and the discussion is decidedly technical.[30] We do not find any evidence that the so-called Aramaisms in the Book of Job indicate any differences in authorship in the various sections of the book. We find virtually no Aramaisms at all. Those that may be Aramaisms are no indication of date, since occasional apparent Aramaisms are found at virtually all strata in the Hebrew language. What the study of the forty-two roots in question does show is, as we would expect, that the author of the Book of Job had a wide vocabulary, wider than that of any other single writer in the Old Testament, except possibly some of the authors whose work is found in Proverbs, and these, after all, were the same type of author and came from the same background.

(e) The use of rare words

There are many words which are found once only in the Hebrew of the Old Testament. There is a preponderance of them in the Book of Job. We have made a count of these *hapax legomena*, and the figures are given in the following table. The first column

[30] See therefore Appendix II.

contains those given in *BDB*. The second column consists of additional words, rediscovered since BDB was published.[31]

No. of Chapters	Section	1	2	Total
6	Elihu: 32-37	17	7	24
4	Job: 3; 29-31	18	6	24
11	1st cycle: 4-14	25	7	32
7	2nd cycle: 15-21	30	13	43
7	Misc.: 22-28	10	13	23
2	Yahweh: 38-39	12	9	21
2	Yahweh: 40-41	13	2	15

We do not find here sufficient variation in any section of the Book of Job to warrant the assumption of a different authorship for any part of the book. We find no such difference of style: that is, in the use of prepositions, in the use of the divine names, in the use of the two first person singular pronouns, in the use of so-called Aramaisms, and in the use of rare words. There is, however, one respect in which we do find a marked difference in style, and this is in the over-elaborated and extra-sophisticated couplets of the Elihu speeches. It is this characteristic which has led critics to say that Elihu is tautologous, and partly also that he is a brash, conceited and cocksure young man. He is indeed a very sure young man, but he is not alone in this, either in his time or in ours. He is also very much out against the orthodoxy of the older men, but again this is a characteristic of the young man in every age. But this is not the whole story. Differences of style are used by Shakespearean critics to show that some of the plays are later than others.[32] We find somewhat similar types of changes in the style of the Elihu speeches compared with the earlier speeches in the

[31] See the later dictionaries, especially that by Koehler and Baumgartner 3rd ed., 1967.

[32] Compare, for instance, *The Tempest* with the earlier plays. That there are differences between an author's earlier work and his later work needs little proof. Compare Scott's *Anne of Geierstein* and *Count Robert of Paris* with (say) *Ivanhoe* or *The Abbot*. Compare Dickens' later novels with his earlier novels. See also R. Gordis, *The Book of God and Man*, p. 110, where he cites the later poems of J. B. Yates, James Joyce's *Finnegan's Wake* and especially Goethe's *Faust* and the differences between the *Urfaust*, the first part which appeared twenty years later, and the second part which appeared twenty years after that. He points out the involved, complicated mode of expression which is characteristic of the second part, and compares it with the epigrammatic style of the first part.

Book of Job. This shows itself in the more precise couplets and in the way in which the author goes to such great pains to produce exact and precise couplets. It is because of this that he incurs the charge of tautology in the Elihu speeches.

We thus find such similarities of style in the Elihu speeches and in the rest of the poetic portions of the Book as lead us to the conclusion that all parts are due to the same author. At the same time we find such differences as to suggest that the author was much older when he wrote the Elihu speeches. What variation of style there is, we find to be in the use of the first person personal pronouns, and this cuts off Job's soliloquy (chs. 3; 29-31) as being different from the rest of the book. This we suppose is because it is the earliest stratum.

We therefore agree with Robert Gordis that the speeches by Elihu are by the same author as the rest of the book. But we disagree with him in his opinion of the way in which the book was built up. We think that the three friends were introduced in the second edition of the book, and that Elihu was introduced in a third and final edition. It is this third edition which is the aged poet's revolt against orthodoxy.

IX

THE SPEECHES OF ELIHU
(*Continued*)

THE section opens with a prose introduction which consists of five verses. It introduces Elihu to the reader. In v. 1 both MT and V refer to 'these three men', but LXX has 'his three friends'. This is assimilating to 2.11 and 32.3, but MT agrees with v. 5. A more important variation is that in v. 1 both MT and V say that the men ceased answering Job because he was 'in the right (*ṣaddīq*) in his own eyes', but S has 'in their eyes', and so also MS 248 in Kennicott's list. This reading means that the three friends gave up the argument because they admitted that Job was in the right. LXX (ἐναντίον αὐτῶν) and Sym (ἐπ' αὐτῶν) make this clear, but make it mean that Job was more in the right than they. Verse 1 can scarcely belong to vv. 2-5, and the MT is right in making a new paragraph begin with v. 2. Verse 1 is an addition to 31.31, and it says that the three men had finished all that they had to say, just as Job had finished what he had to say. We therefore take 32.1 to belong to the second edition of the book (Job and the three friends), and not the third. That is, it was inserted when the three friends came into the story, and not when Elihu came in. This accounts for the difference in style which Dhorme mentions,[1] and it also accounts for the differences between v.1 and vv. 2-5.

Why was Elihu angry? MT says it was because Job has made himself to be more in the right than God (v. 2). This is what LXX says (ἀπέφηνεν, represented himself, proved himself). This is what both V and S say, but it does not agree with v. 1. Also v. 3 says in the Hebrew that Elihu was angry with the three friends because they had found no answer to Job and so put Job in the wrong. This translation does not make sense, and if the Hebrew text is to stand then we must understand it to mean that by not finding an answer to Job and putting him thereby in the wrong, they had actually put him in the right. But we know that the

[1] *Job*, p. 472.

86

present Hebrew text is not the original. It is listed as one of the eighteen changes (*tiqqūn sōpᵉrīm*) deliberately made by the scribes in the interests of orthodoxy. The original statement of MT was that 'they had put God in the wrong'. This helps to explain the strange statement in 42.8 that the three friends had not spoken of God the thing that is true. The passage 42.7f. is dependent on the original of 31.2f. The three friends had not spoken what is true about God and so had put him in the wrong.

The main LXX text follows the present MT text at the end of v. 3 and reads ἀσεβῆ (godless), but there is a LXX reading εὐσεβῆ (pious).² V tries to smooth this out by inserting *tantumodo* (DV, but had only condemned Job). The original MT text presents no difficulties. According to Elihu, both Job and the three friends were in the wrong: Job because he had put himself up against God (33.12); the three friends because they had misrepresented him.

Elihu has been accused of being a conceited, pompous, brash young man. This is mostly because he has spent the whole of ch. 32 in saying that he is now going to speak, that he knows the answers and that he can restrain himself no longer. This indeed overspills into the next chapter to the extent of four or five verses. Elihu is the angry young man who is impatient with the half-solutions of the older generation. He has grown so angry with them all that he can no longer keep quiet. He has remained silent out of respect for the aged, who traditionally in the East have commanded a greater respect than the West knows. And Elihu has come to the conclusion that they are not so very wise after all. It is a conclusion to which every young man comes in every generation, and sometimes he is right. It is certain that the aged love to keep control long after true old age has set in, and often, in the ancient as well as in the modern world, they do keep control. Elihu says that God has not confined wisdom to the aged, but that every man, whatever his age, has the ability and the duty to think things out. It is vv. 18-20 which are mostly responsible for the judgment that Elihu is exhibiting all the characteristics of the cocksure young man. Much of this comment seems to us to be unduly censorious, and the sort of thing the old men themselves would say. We all say these things as we grow old, just as the old men said them of us when we were young. The author has to

² So the fourth corrector of Codex Sin and the corrector of Codex A.

emphasize that Elihu is the young man speaking out, and this we understand to be all the more necessary because by this time the author himself is fighting against the easy and satisfied orthodoxy of the aged. Elihu is saying simply that he cannot keep silent any longer, and that if he does not speak he will burst. He has waited long enough, and now he is going to speak without favour for anybody and, he trusts, without undue disrespect.

The wisdom of the aged has failed. This is the day of the young man.

In ch. 33 Elihu turns to Job and seeks to reply to him on the basis of what Job has already said. The chapter is characterized by a succession of more than ordinarily precise and carefully constructed couplets, almost entirely synonymous, a feature of the author's general style, but apparent especially from ch. 32 onwards.

Many scholars say that there is nothing new in this speech of Elihu's (ch. 33). On the contrary, there is, in our view, something new and quite important. The writer has seen clearly that the real problem of a monotheistic religion is the gap between the immortal and the mortal, between God and humanity, between the High God and the individual man, between the Creator and the creation. This is particularly so when it is realized that in any monotheistic religion the one God must primarily be a High God, removed far from material and earthy things. The critical problem is thus one of communication. How can the High God have any contact with this world in general and with the individual man in particular, and still be a High God? How can lowly and fragile man make any approach whatever to the High God? Elihu knows at least that it is not enough for God to be in high heaven and for man to be bound to the earth. He knows also that the old legend of the Tower of Babel is true; no man can ever build a tower that will reach up to heaven. If therefore there is ever to be any contact between God and man and thus any hope for man, there must be an intercessor: one like enough to God to be able to speak with him, but like enough to man to be able to understand him and speak to him. Thus orthodox monotheistic religions all accept an intermediary—possibly Islam least of all—and some traditions in Christianity assume a whole stairway of intermediaries, intercessors with God, and intercessors with an intercessor with an intercessor.

This necessity of an intermediary was partly recognized in the Angel of God, that special temporary manifestation which appears in the Jahwist and Elchist traditions; for example, in the Samson and in the Gideon traditions as well as in the story of Abraham and the angels who were going to Sodom, but not in either Deuteronomy or in the Priestly tradition. In this chapter we have a different approach, and not a development from the idea of the Angel of God, an idea which by this time had long been abandoned. It is not too much to say that a Christian can, if he wishes, see in these speculations a pre-showing of the incarnation—though if we must talk in this way, we must also say there are pre-showings among peoples independent of these Hebrew-Jewish traditions. But this much is true: here in this chapter the author is seeking to establish a personal link between God and man. He is seeking to bridge that gap which no man can ever bridge. He is seeking to bridge the gap which the High God cannot bridge and still remain a true High God. How can a man of flesh and blood, with all the weaknesses inherent in human nature, weaknesses both physical and moral, with the necessary shortness of human life, bound in the end to return to the dust from which he came—how can this creature ever have any contact with the High God? How can he ever know him or anything of his nature, except on the basis of speculation concerning what is best for himself and for human society? How can a man ever overcome those weaknesses which are born in him, and become triumphant over and after all? The author wonders whether there may be a solution in the current ideas concerning the angels of death.

> What if there were an angel at his side!
> An intermediary, one of a thousand,
> To declare for a man his uprightness.
> Then God might be gracious to him and say:
> 'Turn him back from going down to the death-pit;
> I have found a ransom for him.'
> Then his flesh would recover the plumpness of his youth;
> He would return to the days of his lusty vigour.

LXX has been quite right in interpreting these two verses (33.23f.) in terms of the activity of the angels who are the carriers of the dead, the ἄγγελοι θανατηφόροι, as LXX calls them. Supposing that the death-angel, one of the thousand, who has been sent to carry the dying man away and to escort his spirit to Sheol—supposing this angel were to realize that here is a man undeservedly near to death, and were to take upon himself to declare to God the man's uprightness: would not God then be gracious and turn the man back to life again, declaring to all that he has found a good reason for releasing the man from the bonds of oncoming death and bringing him back to full and vigorous life? Elihu (or better, the author) has thought of a being who might possibly be an intermediary between the High God and man. This angel of death could be the mediator, the ombudsman, for whom Job has been longing and searching all along.

In ch. 34, after the usual introduction, Elihu deals with Job's claim that he is righteous. He says that God is certainly not wicked. In suggesting that God does act wickedly or that he gives tacit consent to the triumph of the wicked, Job is going from bad to worse. He is adding rebellion to error.

Chapter 35 is shorter than the others and has no preliminary couplets of the type with which the speeches normally begin. Here the speaker plunges straight into the argument. He says two things. The first is: God is not benefited either by man's goodness or by man's badness. Why then should he favour anybody? This is why you can be sure that God is really and truly just. He has nothing to gain by being unjust. The second thing is: when men cry to God for help, they often appeal to him for the wrong reason. This is why they get no answer.

Chapter 36 opens with a different introduction: 'and Elihu added and said', though LXX has the same phrasing as elsewhere: 35.1; 34.1; 33.31 (codex A), etc. There are three couplets of an introductory nature, where Elihu says that he has more to say, and that he can solve the problem. In our judgment these three couplets are not bombastic, except in so far as age in every generation tends to resent the certainty and the confidence of youth. Particularly, these verses are not bombastic if we accept that the author thought that the young man has more to say that is worth while saying than have the adherents of the old orthodoxy. It is true that Elihu talks a great deal, but there is considerable justification for saying that some of the most original thoughts in the book are to be found in these chapters. It is not surprising that Budde thought that the author from the start intended the solution to be found here. Modern writers rightly claim that the author of the Book of Job was a literary artist of some considerable skill.

In this case there is no reason to suppose that he could not have invented a real character like Elihu, the young man who starts by being diffident in the presence of his elders, but all the more confident and full of talk when once he gets started. Elihu is at least as real a character as Job is, and very much more so than any of the three friends, even more than Eliphaz who is the most convincing of the three as a character. For the most part, the three friends are very little more than dummies, stooges, and the general orthodox featurelessness of their speeches is one reason why the scholars differ so much when they seek to redistribute the content of chs. 24-27 among them in order to create a third cycle similar to the other two. But Elihu's speeches can belong to nobody but Elihu, and this is true of almost every couplet in the six chapters. Here in chs. 36 and 37 we have Elihu's final words. Hitherto he has mentioned more than one subsidiary problem. Here he seeks to deal with the basic problem of the book: the problem of the ways of the High God with mankind, and in particular the problem of how God's righteousness is manifested here on earth.

No man can approach God, shrouded as he is in mystery and awful splendour. We must fear him with holy awe, and accept his sovereign dictates.

X

THE AIMS OF THE AUTHOR

WHY did the author of the Book of Job write this book? What did he want to say?

Our thesis is that he developed his thought and his theme in three stages. His first intention was to tell a story in Hebrew comparable with the story of the Babylonian Job, a normal and orthodox piece of wisdom literature, with observations on real life, but with no particular theorizing about them. He rewrote the ancient folk-tale of the righteous Job in a traditional form, inserting a long poetic piece into a prose tale. This was the normal practice of these wisdom writers. The prose tale consisted of a prologue and an epilogue. The poetic piece contained a long soliloquy by Job followed by a speech by God. Job first apologizes for having spoken at all and finally surrenders in complete humility, acknowledging his ignorance in abject repentance. The teaching of this first edition of the book is that man can do no other than submit to his fate. God knows what he is doing, and if man in his weakness and ignorance submits, then all will be doubly well in the end. The author is following a general and well-established pattern, but he has a particular model, and this model was the Babylonian Job.

In the prose sections of the first edition we have the story of a desert sheik who was entirely prosperous. He had considerable property, all in live-stock,[1] many retainers, and a grown-up family of seven sons and three daughters, with all the seven sons having each his own establishment. The man Job was conscientiously righteous, and he would go to all lengths to do what is right and fitting. He meets with a double series of disasters and is reduced to abject poverty and extreme sickness. His wife urges him to 'renounce God and die', but he maintains his integrity. Nothing that has happened has made the slightest difference to him in his principles or in the way he sought to put them into practice. He submits to the divine will, and he continues to adopt this attitude

[1] Cf. the original meaning of the Hebrew *miqneh*, property in cattle.

in spite of everything his wife says. 'Shall we receive good at the hand of God, and shall we not receive evil?' In the poetic inset Job bemoans his sad lot (ch. 3). There is no discussion of the hard lot of mankind in general, and nothing about the relation of God to that problem. In ch. 29 we have a picture of Job's former prosperity, but now we see not the Job of the folk-tale, who is the traditional wealthy desert sheik, but the leading citizen of a settled community. The archaic setting is still present, but now it is similar to that of the Book of Ruth. Job is the leading citizen, and his position is similar to that of Boaz, though more splendid. The chapter is a factual description of the kind of life which such a venerated leader of the community was thought to have led in days gone by. Chapter 30 is a similar factual account, but this time of Job's subsequent distress. Once again there is no charge made against God. It is simply that, as a matter of fact, Job looked for good fortune, but found bad fortune (v. 26). In ch. 31 Job swears on oath that he is innocent. Step by step he goes through a long list of possible omissions and commissions. This is the kind of thing which we have found elsewhere in early wisdom literature. Let his accuser write down the indictment and Job will be proud to carry it himself. He is quite willing to have his whole life made public and to submit to the verdict. This is the end of what Job has to say. No problem is discussed. Job is sure that something has gone wrong somewhere, but he ascribes no blame. In the Yahweh speeches we have two stages, one in each speech. The first speech emphasizes man's weakness and ineptitude. Job, no more than any other human being, cannot control the great forces of nature (ch. 38), nor can he control the wild creatures that range freely where they will (ch. 39). Job recognizes his weakness, apologizes for having spoken and will say no more. In the second speech Yahweh demonstrates his supreme power, giving two particular instances of semi-mythical creatures of travellers' tales. In the end Job submits with complete humility. And so to the epilogue where all ends more than happily. The relations all crowd round. Job dies at last in a happy and blessed old age, having seen sons and sons' sons and even sons' sons' sons around him.

All here is perfectly orthodox. But the author came to have further thoughts. This is the second stage in the development of his thought. After all, there is a problem here. It is not enough to say that God knows all and therefore knows best, and that we must submit to him, assured that everything will turn out all right at last. It is such a long 'at last'. The fact of experience is that everything does not turn out well at last, perhaps never, but certainly often not in a man's lifetime. Often it turns out wrong, and the wrong individuals suffer. Why is it that God allows this kind of thing to happen? What sort of a God is it that allows this kind of thing to happen? Does he really know what is happening? If he does know, does he care? Or, is it the case that he does not know what is happening? Or is he simply capricious? In fact, can the old orthodoxy really be defended? And further, if God in his wisdom has seen fit to give men brains and the ability to use them, why should man be prohibited from using his brains in relation to the very things which touch him most nearly?

So we come to the second edition of Job, the edition which included the three friends. These three friends are all thoroughly orthodox. They represent the aged wise men. They say all that there is to be said for the orthodox position about God and suffering, and they say it many, many times. Here in the dialogue the author adopts an attitude different from that in the first edition (chs. 3; 29-31; 38-41). In the first edition he had done nothing more than give an account of Job's present distress, his former greatness, his present humiliation, and his statement on oath that he is innocent. But in the dialogue the question is asked: why has Job suffered so much? The immediate problem is the suffering of this one righteous man. It is all very well, says Job, for the three friends to keep on saying that the righteous prosper and the wicked come to a bad end, or to say (under pressure) that if the wicked do indeed prosper, it is only for a short while and their end will come suddenly and disastrously. Job says that this just is not so. To say a thing twice does not establish it as a fact for the three friends any more than for Humpty Dumpty. Job challenges the statements of the three friends which they have made in the interests of orthodox belief. He himself, however, is still as orthodox as ever. He believes that there is an answer to the problem, and that if once he gets through to the presence of the High God, then all will be well.

But it is necessary to notice the arguments of the three friends. The argument in Eliphaz's first speech is based on the unique, absolute power of the High God. He claims to have had a supernatural vision to confirm the statement that God is bound to be in the right. Not even the very angels in heaven can put him in the wrong. If Job will turn to this High God, place the whole matter before him, then all will be well. He gives two reasons for this: the first is that God loves to exalt the lowly and to bring down the proud. This again is an argument based not on the right and wrong of things, but on the gracious condescension of the High God. The second reason is a variation of the orthodox view that any suffering is bound to be temporary: pain and trouble are a discipline. The other two friends are virtually make-weights so far as this first cycle is concerned. Bildad (ch. 8) adds very little. It is all rubbish to say that God Almighty is guilty of injustice. Seek his favour and all will be well. Zophar (ch. 11) has little sympathy with Job. He tells Job that he is being let off lightly. Let him put his iniquity away, and all will be well. The fact that the orthodox position depends on the supreme power of the High God is very clear here. If only God would declare his wisdom and efficiency (*tūšiyā*)! Verses 7-10 emphasize this unapproachable nature of God. Man is no good at all: and stupid man will get sense when a wild-ass colt is born human!

Thus quickly the main basis of the argument has turned into the problem of the High God. Job needs to put his case before God. The whole matter turns on this. How can he get into touch with God? And if he can get in touch with him, then how can he get anything like a fair hearing before this awful High God? What difference does it make to God whether Job has sinned or not? Here we have one of the corollaries of a belief in a High God. He is so remote, so perfect, so self-sufficient that nothing any man may do, either way, can affect him at all.

No: it is not possible for Job to do as the friends suggest and as he himself desired. He cannot approach God even to sue as a suppliant: let alone state his case. God is too powerful and too awesome. He destroys good and bad indiscriminately. If only there could be some sort of umpire to see fair play. This is another corollary of a belief in such a High God: there must be some buffer between God and man. Yet again (ch. 10), how can it benefit God to oppress a man or to prosper a man? Why should God bother either way? Why should God search for Job's sin? Further, what an extraordinary business it is that God should go to all the trouble to make a man and then treat him like this. Then in ch. 12 (which we take to be part of the closing speech of the first cycle) Job says: the man who calls on God, innocent though he is and innocent though I am, gets his answer all right, but it is not the answer the orthodox gives! But in ch. 13 we get another aspect of the problem. If God is so absolutely pure, then no godless man could possibly appear before him. God is so supremely righteous that nothing unrighteous can ever come into his presence. Therefore, if Job did manage to appear before God, he would already have won his case. That very appearance would prove that he was righteous. Again, if Job is ever to get his case heard, the High God will have to 'turn off' the blasting terror of his presence.

In the second cycle (14.13) Job has a sudden bright idea. It is a way of getting rid of the suffering and getting things put right without his appearing before God at all. What if a man could 'duck', die and yet live? This has nothing to do with any idea of immortality, and it has nothing to do with any idea of a resurrection from the dead. Supposing a man could be hidden till all the troubles were over: not die and come to life again, but hide and then be called out of hiding. But Job quickly turns away from such an extravagant suggestion. The three friends continue in this second cycle with their exemplary orthodoxy. Eliphaz says that God is supreme in heaven above and even more so on the earth below. He produces the charge of the orthodox establishment of every age. Whoever attacks the established orthodoxy is accused of destroying religion. In this second cycle Job is mostly concerned with this matter of getting a hearing before the mighty and supreme High God. All the time we are getting farther and farther away from the Job of the prologue with his disasters and sickness which virtually are 'acts of God'. We are also getting farther away from the Job of the soliloquy (chs. 3; 29-31). In 19.6 Job claims that God has put him in the wrong. He can get no answer and there is no justice. But (19.23-27b) Job is sure that one day his vindicator will stand up as a witness beside him and that with joy he (Job) will see God, see him with his own eyes—and then suddenly (v. 27c) his heart fails him.

Strictly, the third cycle (21.22-27.23) is non-existent, though the normal scheme is partially followed as far as 25.6. But, as we have seen, the sentiments of the first two cycles are ascribed indiscriminately to all four speakers. Eliphaz says what Job has said. Job says what the others say. Bildad says what Job has said, and Zophar says nothing at all.[2] We find statements concerning the isolation and unconcern of the High God (22.3). If he is beyond the clouds, how can he see to do anything (22.13f)? The same isolation is found in ch. 23 where Job says that he is sure that if only he could reach God, then God would listen; but he cannot find God. Thick darkness obscures him. According to ch. 25 God is all-powerful and man can do nothing. But otherwise, these chapters are in such confusion that we cannot base any assessment of what the various characters say on what is found here.

The net result of the dialogue is that God does nothing about the injustice which is in the world. He cannot see; he does not know. Or if he does see and know, he is too far removed from this world of mortal man to do anything: he is too pure and holy to have anything to do with sin. There is no way in which a man can ever get near enough to the High God in order to have his case heard and get justice. Except for this: at the end of the dialogue, in ch. 28, and at the end of the chapter as though a summary of it, there is a practical solution. What is required above all, in heaven, on earth, throughout all creation is *ḥokmā* (wisdom, shrewdness), and *bīnā* (understanding) with the resultant *tūšiyyā* (efficiency). All this belongs to God alone, and man can never find it. It is inevitably and for ever beyond man's reach. But God has provided a practical solution. For man it means 'Fear God and turn away from evil'. This is our wisdom here below. The verse comes at the end of the verse addition which formed the second edition of the book, and probably it was intentionally placed there.

The author of the Book of Job is not satisfied with his solution. It is true that 28.28 is enough to be going on with, and that it is a safe guide for man, but the problem of the gap between the High God and mortal man remains. This must be solved. Elihu, the angry young man, appears in ch. 32 and sets out to put everybody right. As the sequel shows, he has some bright suggestions (especially one of them), but he has no solution. Chapter 32 is the young man seeking to justify his intervention in a world where only the aged may speak. His action needs a great deal of justifying, for his was a world in which silence before the aged was a rule

---

[2] The attempts of the scholars to straighten all this out are to be seen in Appendix I.

incomprehensible to our modern world, and far more absolute than what modern people can understand. In ch. 33 Elihu says: God does not bandy words. He does not argue. He says what he has to say once in man's secret ear, and that is that. He does not repeat himself; he does not explain himself. He speaks, and that is the end of it. This is why Job is wrong to expect to enter into discussion with him. God does not answer questions. But here we find one of Elihu's suggestions (33.23-28). If there is to be any coming-together (at-one-ment) between God and man, then there must be an intermediary, some being who is 'betwixt and between' so far as God and men are concerned. What about one of the death-carrying angels, those who come just before the moment of death to carry the spirit away to Sheol? What if this angel, almost at the moment of death, should see that the man is innocent and does not deserve to die for any sin, and should thereupon intercede with the High God to allow him to regain the full vigour of his youth?

In ch. 33 Elihu says that there must be an all-powerful High God, one who cannot act wickedly. You cannot have an irresponsible person running a nation. In the same way you have to have a High God to run the whole world. And if sometimes on earth you get tyranny and injustice, Elihu says that there are times when God allows a godless man to be king in order to punish the people. Which, perhaps, is Elihu's way of saying that people get the kind of government they deserve. In ch. 34 we find another approach, and once more (as in the case of the necessary intermediary) it provides a useful line of thought. Nothing a man can do, can affect God, whether it is good or bad. But it can and does affect a man. In one way this is not a new suggestion in the book; see 5.6f.—man stirs up his own trouble for himself; affliction does not happen automatically. But Elihu's remark does open the way to the idea of a natural and inevitable retribution which God has built in to the nature of things. It is along some such line as this that the incidence of suffering can be understood.

In ch. 36 Elihu does some straight talking. Take kings on their thrones, for instance. God makes them secure on their thrones and then they become arrogant. That is when trouble may come. They get their warning. If they repent and mend their ways, then they end their days in affluence. If they do not mend their ways, then they die. And that, says Elihu to Job, is what is wrong with you. God is greater than you are. Give him the credit for it, and be willing to learn from him. Elihu has no solution, and ch. 37 concludes with: God is all-powerful. What we have to do is to reverence him, and believe that he is the Lord[3] of righteousness. He is not to be gainsaid.[4]

Thus the author has no solution for his problem of how there can be any contact between the High God and lowly man. He has a practical solution, one which provides a proper way of life, but the problem is still there. 'Trust and obey' is a sound enough way of life, but man is so built that he must keep on trying to make sense of things. The Jews sought in the end to solve the problem of the necessary intermediary by exalting the Law. The Greeks had their Logos. And both had their galaxy of angels and heavenly spirits. Christianity supplies the 'impossible' solution in the incarnation. But has *orthodox* Christianity indeed solved the problem? Orthodoxy still retains the idea of the High God, and Christians find it necessary to have a whole range of intermediaries, the God-man, semi-divine creatures, human intercessors—all in spite of I Tim. 2.5: 'one mediator also between God and men, himself man, Christ Jesus'. But is this right? Ought it to be 'himself God' or 'himself God and himself man'? But all this, quite definitely, 'is another story'.

[3] Read *rab*.   [4] Read the root '*nh* I.

APPENDIX I

THE following are some of the reconstructions of chs. 24-27 and
29-31 which have been proposed in order to obtain a third cycle
of speeches comparable with the other two. See, in part, the list
in R. H. Pfeiffer, *Introduction to the Old Testament*, pp. 671ff.

Kennicott.
Eliphaz and *Job* as in the text; *Eliphaz*: 22. *Job*: 23-24.
Bildad: 25. *Job*: 26; 27.1-12.
Zophar: 27.13-23. *Job*: 28-31.

Stuhlmann.
Eliphaz and *Job* as in the text.
Bildad: 25; 28. *Job*: 26; 27.1-10.
Zophar: 27.11-23. *Job*: 29-31.

Reuss.
Eliphaz and *Job* as in the text.
Bildad: 25; 26.5-14. *Job*: 26.1-4; 27.1-12.
Zophar: ? 27.13-23. *Job*: 29-31; 28 interpolated.

Hoffmann.
Eliphaz and *Job* as in text.
Bildad: 25; 24.13-25. *Job*: 26.1-27.6.
Zophar: 27.7-28.28. *Job*: 29-31.

Bickell.
Eliphaz and *Job* as text.
Bildad: 25.1-3; 26.12-13; 26.14c; 25.4-6; 28. *Job*: 26.1-4; 27.2-6;
    27.11f; 28.
Zophar: 27.7-10, 14-23. *Job*: 29-31.

Duhm.
Bildad: 25.1; 26.1-4; 25.2-6; 26.5-14. *Job*: 26.1; 27.2-6, 12.
Zophar: 27.7-11, 13-23. *Job*: 29-31.
But 24.1-24; 28; 30.1-8 are interpolations. This may well mean
that Duhm found himself unable to allocate these verses, especi-
ally those in chs. 24 and 30, to any of the four speakers, and

therefore was compelled to fall back on the idea of interpolations.

Siegfried.
Bildad: 25; 26.5-14. *Job*. 26.1-14; 27.2-6; 29-31.
He regarded 27.7-28.28 as an interpolation, and did not seek to establish a full third cycle.

Laue.
Eliphaz and *Job* as text.
Bildad: 26.13-23. *Job*: 26.1-3; 9.2-24.
Zophar: 28. *Job*: 12; 26.1-6 (genuine, but place uncertain).

Gordis:
Eliphaz and *Job* as text.
Bildad: 25; 26.5-14. *Job*: 27.1-4; 27.1-12.
Zophar: 27.13-23. Only this has survived of Zophar's speech, and nothing of Job's reply.

Peake.
Eliphaz and *Job* as in text.
Bildad: 25.1-6; 25.5-14. *Job*: 26.1-4; 27.2-6, 11, 12.
Zophar: 24.18-21; 27.7-10, 12-23. *Job*: 29-31.

Driver-Gray.
Eliphaz and *Job* as in text.
Bildad: 25; ? 26. *Job*: 27.2-6, 11f.
Zophar:? 27.7-10, 13-23.

Buhl.
'24-28'. All fragments of varied origin.

Kissane.
Eliphaz and *Job*. as in text.
Bildad: 26.1-4; 27.7-23. *Job*: 29-30.
Zophar: 25; 26.5-14. *Job*: 27.1-6; 31.

Lefèvre.
Eliphaz: 22. *Job*: 23.1-24.17.
Bildad: 26.5-14; 25.2-6. *Job*: 26.2-4; 27.2-12.
Zophar: 27.13-23; 24.18-25.

Tournay.
Eliphaz and *Job* as in text, as far as 24.17.
Bildad: 26.5-14; 25.2-26.4. *Job*: 27.1-12.
Zophar: 27.13-23; 24.18-25.

Hertzberg.
Bildad: 23.13-24; 25.2-6. *Job*: 26.1-4; 27.11f; 26.5-14; 27.2-6.
Zophar: 27.7-10, 13-23.

Marshall.
Zophar: 25.2-6; 26.5-14.

Hölscher.
Bildad: 25.1; 26.2-4; 25.2-6; 26.5-14. *Job*: 26.1-12.
Zophar: 17.13-23.

Stevenson.
Bildad: 25 (opening); 26.5-14 (less easily identified). *Job*: 26.2-4;
    27.2-6, 11-13, 22.
Zophar: 27.7-10, 13-21, 23.

Lindblom.
Bildad: 25; 26.5-14. *Job*. 26.1-4; 27.2-10.
Zophar: 26.13-23.

Levy.
Bildad: 25.1-5; 24.18-20; 27.13-23.

Terrien.
Eliphaz: 22.1-30. *Job*. 23.1-17; 24.1-17, 25.
Bildad: 25.1-6; 26.5-14. *Job*. 26.1-4; 27.1-12.
Zophar: 24.18-24; 27.17-23. *Job*: censored.

Dhorme.
Eliphaz: 22. *Job*: 23.1-24.17; 24.25.
Bildad: 26.5-14; 25. *Job*: 26.1-4; 27.2-12.
Zophar: 24.18-24; 27.13-23. *Job*: (28); 29-31.

Fohrer.
Bildad: 25. *Job*: 26.1-4; 27.1-6, 11-12.
All the rest, from 24 onwards, is composed on separate songs.

G. A. Barton and even more Buttenweiser and Torczyner, have
made proposals of readjustment of considerable complexity; as
also Dhorme. Fullerton thinks that chs. 21-31 have been tampered
with in many places in dogmatic interests. Many scholars regard
parts of these chapters as interpolations, presumably we would
say because they did not know to whom to allocate them any
more than the author knew. Laue omits 25. Grill omits 26-27.1.
Studer omits 27.7-28.28, and so also Kuenen. Duhm omits 24.1-24;

28.30.1-8. Cheyne regards 20.28 as secondary. Baumgärtel finds very little original (i.e. belonging to the first author) after 13 (only 16.6, 9, 12-21; 19.2-29; 22.2-7, 10-17; 31.35, 37). Kraeling finds only remnants of a third cycle: 33.2-7, 10-17; 30.16-31; 31.35, 37.

APPENDIX II

THIS is a discussion of the so-called Aramaisms in the Book of Job. There is a discussion of these in the article by A. Guillaume, 'The Unity of the Book of Job', *The Annual of the Leeds University Oriental Society*, IV (1964), pp. 26-46. We follow the classification and the order in which the roots are cited in Driver-Gray, *Job*, ICC, pp. xlvi-xlvii. We hold that if a root is found elsewhere than in Aramaic, and if the transformation rules concerning the consonants are observed, then the word is not an Aramaism. It is, we maintain, a rare word which has been retained in the memory of the literary writers, those who were the wise men of Israel, those who had pretensions to culture and who were aware of the literature of the other countries of the Fertile Crescent.

First we deal with the so-called Aramaisms found throughout the book; i.e. both in the Elihu speeches and in the remainder of the book.

1. *'lp* (*piel*, teach). It is found three times in the Book of Job: 33.33; 35.11 in Elihu, and 15.5 in the rest. Elsewhere it is found only in the *qal*, Prov. 22.25 (learn). Aramaic *'ᵃlap*, Syriac *yilep* (learn); Syriac *yallep* (teach). See also Arabic *'alifa* (be familiar with) and *muta'allaf* (trained). The meaning 'be familiar with' is found in the Targums. Outside the wisdom literature, the Hebrew root means 'tame' (Hebrew *'allūp*, Arabic *'alūf*) and 'friend, intimate companion' (Hebrew *'allūp*, Arabic *'ilf*). The Syriac *yalīpūtā* means 'knowledge'. The word is a good Semitic root, and a perfectly good Hebrew root. The author of the Book of Job had three words for 'teach': the *hiphil* of *yrh* (five times, Prov. 2), the *hiphil* of *bīn* (3 times, Prov. 10), and the *piel* of *'lp* (twice and none). The difference between *yrh* and *'lp* is that from Deuteronomy onwards *yrh* gradually became more and more associated with 'authoritative direction given by the priests on matters of ceremonial observance '(BDB, 435b), and *'lp* became associated with the teaching of wisdom. *'lp* is the regular word used in the Targums and the Talmud for 'teach', whereas the *hiphil* of *yrh* is used

regularly of legalistic decisions and what we would call 'counsel's opinions'.

2. *ḥwh* (tell, declare). It is found three times in the Book of Job, Elihu in 32.10, 17; 36.2; rest, 15.17. Elsewhere it is found in Ps. 19.3 and (possibly) 52.11. Aramaic *ḥawwey*; Syriac *ḥawwiy*, Targums and both Talmuds. But it is also found in Arabic: *ḥawa'* (sound). Two of the three cases in the Elihu speeches are in ch. 32, the chapter in which Elihu says again and again that he has something to say and he can wait no longer. The subject matter thus involves extra use of such a root as this, and to that extent the strength of the argument based on its greater frequency in the Elihu speeches is diminished. We take this to be a true Hebrew root. The noun *'aḥwā* (13.17) is said to be an Aramaic *aphel* infinitive formation, but is this so? It could be *'aḥwāyā*, and there are nouns in Hebrew with prosthetic *aleph* (GK, 85*b*). Also LXX here has ἀναγγελῶ, which represents *'aḥawweh*, the *piel* of the verb.

3. *mll* (speak). The verb is found in 8.2, and in Elihu 33.3; also Gen. 21.7 and Ps. 106.2. The noun is found thirty-four times in Job (fourteen in Elihu) and four times elsewhere. There is thus a marked preponderance in Job. The root is common in the Targums, in Aramaic and in Syriac, but see also the Arabic *malla* (IV form, dictate a letter). Nöldeke maintained that it is a perfectly good Hebrew root. The occurrence in Gen. 21.7 is impressive.

4. *śg', śgh* (grow great). The root with *aleph* is found only in Job; 12.23 and in Elihu 36.24; and the adjective with *aleph* in Job 36.26; 37.23 only. The root with *he* is found in Job 8.7, 11 and in Pss. 73.12; 92.13. The two forms, one with *aleph* and one with *yodh*, are found in Aramaic. Both roots are Aramaisms, but the occurrences of the *he*-root in the Psalms minimizes the importance of this. In any case, the use of this root in the Elihu speech is no evidence of diverse authorship.

Secondly we deal with roots which are found in the Book of Job, but not in the Elihu speeches.

5. The noun *'aḥwā*: see above, 2.

6. *hēn* (if). The difference between *hēn* (behold) and *hēn* (if) is sometimes most difficult to detect; cf. Ex. 4.1. It is held that *hēn*

(if) occurs six times in Job and six times elsewhere, but it is used at all periods (Ex. 4.1; 8.22, etc.). Here is another instance which shows that an occasional so-called Aramaism is not a sign of lateness. It is liable to be found at any period, and the difference between *hēn* (behold) and *hēn* (if) may be a matter of the way in which the word is spoken; cf. the English word 'surely'.

7. *ḥdh* (rejoice); It is found in Job 3.6, but also in Ex. 18.9 (Elohist tradition); I Sam. 6.19 (see LXX); Ps. 21.7; Aramaic and Syriac *ḥ*ᵃ*da*, Accadian *ḥadū*; Ugarit *ḥdw* (A III 6.6; B V 5.22). It is difficult to see why this root should ever have been called an Aramaism. It is a perfectly good general Semitic root. If this root is an Aramaism, then Aramaisms were part of the Hebrew language from a comparatively early time, and the whole point of isolating them fails.

8. *ṭūś* (rush, dart). It is found in Job 9.26; nowhere else. Aramaic *ṭūs*, Syriac *ṭās*. Jastrow indicates that the root is used chiefly of the swift flight of birds. The root is called an Aramaism only because it has not been found elsewhere in Hebrew.

9. *ṭpl* (smear, plaster). It is found in Job 13.4; 14.17; Ps. 119.69. Aramaic *ṭ*ᵉ*pal*, Syriac *ṭappel* (defile), ? Accadian *ṭapālu* (besmear), Arabic *ṭafīla* (of a plant being soiled by mud) and *ṭafal* (dried mud). The word is not an Aramaism; cf. Guillaume, *Abr Nahraim* III 17.

10. *yqr* (splendid). It is found in 31.26. Aramaic *y*ᵉ*qar*, Syriac *yiqar*, Accadian *aqaru* (splendid, glorious, heavy). The original meaning is 'be heavy' (Arabic *waqara*) with a development similar to that of the root *kbd*, for which it is at all levels a good synonym. But there is also another line of development, cf. Arabic (dignity, calm). The meaning here in 31.26 is probably the 'calm splendour' of the full moon. The word here therefore is closer to Arabic than to Aramaic. It is not an Aramaism, but a regular Hebrew root with a whole range of meanings.

11. *kēp* (rock), 30.6 and Jer. 4.29. This is well-known in Aramaic and Syriac, but it is found also in Assadian *kāpu*. We see no reason why it should not be recognized as a true Hebrew word, though rarely found in extant literature. Whether it was common in ancient time, in speech or in writing or in both, it is not possible to say.

12. *kāpān* (hunger, famine), 5.22; 30.3. Aramaic *kᵉpen* and *kᵉpēn* (be hungry), Syriac *kᵉpen* (be hungry). The Arabic *kafana* means 'spin (wool), cover (bread) with hot ashes', and *kaffana* is 'enshroud a corpse', *kafan* is 'shroud'. In Ezek. 17.7 the verb is used of a vine reaching out with its roots. Probably, therefore, the root primarily is 'reach out', with 'eager for' as a development; cf. *Genesis Rabba* p. 79 and its reference to Job 5.22. A further development is 'eager for food' and so to 'be hungry for', and this is as legitimate a development in Hebrew as 'enveloping, covering' is in Arabic.

13. *lāhēn*, 30.24. Both text and word are too uncertain to be used as evidence for anything. The best texts read *lāhen*.

14. *mkk* (be low, humiliated), 24.24; Ps. 106.43; Eccles. 10.18. Aramaic *mᵉkak*, Syraic *makk* (be low), Ugarit *mkk* (sink down: B III* A 17). Arabic *makka* (suck out entirely, diminish). Guillaume quotes the Arabic *makka ruḥahu* (he crushed his spirit). The word is a perfectly good general Semitic root, and belongs to Hebrew as much as to the rest.

15. *nḥt* (descend), 21.13, but also Prov. 17.10; Jer. 21.13; Pss. 38.3; 18.35 (II Sam. 22.35); Joel 4.11. If this root is an Aramaism, then Aramaisms are so much part of the language that it is a waste of time arguing about them. The noun is found in Isa. 30.30 and perhaps the adjective in II Kings 6.9. Aramaic and Syriac *nᵉḥat*, common in the Targums and the Talmud, Ugarit *nḥt* (B III* A 11, 18; S ii 3, ii 6, 9, 13). Guillaume quotes the form *inḥatta* (fell). The root is poetic in Hebrew, and Nöldeke rightly recognized it as a perfectly good Hebrew root.

16. *'ārôd* (wild ass), 39.5. Aramaic and Syriac *'ᵃrādâ*, also the Targums and the Talmud. The corresponding Arabic root is not *'arada* with the light *ayin* (flee away), but *ġarada* with the heavy *ayin* (bray, of the wild ass), D. H. Moeller. Whoever has heard the braying of wild asses at night requires no further argument. The word is a perfectly good Hebrew word (Nöldeke), and a good, though rare synonym of the more common *pere'*. If the Hebrew poets had had as much occasion to refer to the wild ass as to the lion, it is probable that the 'braying' (root *'rd*) of the ass would have been as common in extant Hebrew literature as the 'roaring' (root *š'g*) of the lion.

17. *'tq* (advanced in years), 21.7 and Ps. 6.8 (of the eye, growing old and weak). The more usual Hebrew meaning is 'move on, proceed', but in Prov. 25.1 the meaning is 'transcribe' (i.e. proceed from one scroll to another), and so LXX, Vulgate and often in later Hebrew. In modern Hebrew *he 'tíq* means 'copy, translate, remove'. The meaning 'move' is found in Job 14.18, 18.4, and 'advance' in 9.5. It is true that most often 'grow old' is the meaning in Aramaic and Syriac, but the root also means 'remain long, settle permanently'. The meaning 'move, advance' is found in the Accadian *etēqu*, but in Ugarit the meaning is 'pass away, change' (B III 2.26, K II 1.5, Virolleaud; K II 1.2, 16, Ginsberg). The Arabic *'ataqa* (*'atuqa*) is 'proceed, pass forth, become free, grow old'. We judge that 'grow old' (cf. English 'getting on') is a normal development in any language, and we see no reason why this should not have taken place in Hebrew equally as in any other language.

18. *'aštût* (thought), 12.5, unless the word is a plural *'ašātōt* from a form *'ešet*. The verb is found in Jonah 1.6 and the noun *'eštōnā* in Ps. 146.4; cf. Ecclus. 3.23. The root had originally to do with the forging of metal (*'ešet*, wrought metal, a metal bar: so Mishnah and the early Midrashim; cf. modern Hebrew) and thence 'plan, think out'. The root is certainly late Hebrew, but not so certainly Aramaic.

19. *qbl* (receive, take), 2.10 *bis*, but also Esther 4.4; Prov. 19.20; five times in the Chronicler, and twice (26.5; 36.12 Priestly tradition) in Exodus meaning 'oppositeness'. It is indeed a common Aramaic root, but the meaning 'accept' is found also in Arabic (*qabala*), in Ethiopic and in Ugarit (A II 5.34). The root may be late in Hebrew rather than early, but it is Hebrew.

20. *qᵉrāb* (war, battle), 38.23 and six (seven ?) times elsewhere. As Nöldeke (pp. 413f.) pointed out, the traditional vowels are Aramaic, but this is not necessarily the original Hebrew vowelling; cf. the plural in Ps. 68.31. The use of the root to mean *hostile* approach may be a somewhat late development in Hebrew, but it is Hebrew. The Arabic root, like the Hebrew root, branches out in all directions.

21. *šāhēd* (witness), 16.19 and the Aramaic in Gen. 31.47. Aramaic and Syriac *sᵉhad* with *samech*; Arabic *šahida* (testify) and *šāhid*

(witness) with *shin*. These are perfectly good transformations. The word is a perfectly good Hebrew word, and a synonym for the usual *'ēd*.

22. *šerīrīm*, 40.16. Both LXX and the Vulgate understood this word to mean 'navel'; cf. Arabic *surrat* and *sur*, Syriac *serra*. The Arabic *surriyat* means 'concubine, female slave', so the word may mean 'private parts'. The transformation of the sibilant is regular, and the word is a good Hebrew formation.

23. *tqp* (prevail over, overpower), 14.20; 15.24 and Eccles. 4.12. The root is certainly common in Aramaic and Syriac, but Arabic *taqifa* is 'overpower', and the word may well be truly Hebrew.

Thirdly we come to the following words found, so far as the Book of Job is concerned, only in the Elihu speeches.

24. *bḥr* (test), 34.4. This meaning predominates in Aramaic, but it is sometimes difficult to decide whether the meaning is 'choose' or 'test'. Cf. Isa. 48.10 where LXX and the Targum have 'test' and the Vulgate and the Rabbis have 'choose'. Both make good sense. The Arabic *tabaḥḥar* means 'test thoroughly' and *baḥara* means 'till the earth', whence 'cleave, penetrate, examine, choose'. We do not find that the meaning 'test' is necessarily an Aramaism, though it may well be.

25. *ḥap* (clean), 33.9. Nöldeke (p. 415) says that the meaning required here is not found in Aramaic. The meaning is 'scrape, rub, cleanse the head' and the Syriac *ḥepāpā* has to do with soaping, shampooing, cleansing. The Arabic *ḥipap* is a border of hair round a bald head, whence 'rim, border' of any kind. Apparently the word primarily involved the head being bare except only for a fringe all round, whence the root developed to mean 'bald, clean'. The word is a good, though rare, Hebrew word.

26. *ktr*, 36.2. This is said to be an Aramaism and to mean 'wait (for me)', cf. LXX μεῖνόν με and the Vulgate *sustine me*. This meaning is common in Syriac but rare in Aramaic. The normal Hebrew meaning is 'surround' (Judg. 20.43 and Ps. 22.13, where the parallel is *sbb*, Hab. 1.4). Jastrow gives a meaning 'knot a tie' which we understand to mean tying something round the neck. Also *katr* is the hump of a camel and *kitr* is any domelike structure.

We take the verb in Hebrew to mean 'gather round expectantly' (*BDB* 509b) and the LXX translation could presuppose this. We find no Aramaism here.

27. *ma'bād*, 34.25. The pointing is late Hebrew and probably influenced by Aramaic. But, as in the case of *q*e*rāb* (see above, 18), it may not have been the original pointing.

28. *'qb*, 37.4. This is said to be an Aramaism, but only because the versions could make nothing of it, and commentators have supposed it to be an error for, or a variation of, the root *'kb* (hold back). But we understand the root to be the normal *'qb* (follow at the heel) and so 'follow immediately'.

29. *r"* (break), 34.24 and five (six) times outside the Book of Job. This root is an Aramaism; it occurs not only in the Elihu speeches, but sporadically everywhere in the Old Testament: Jer. 11.16; 15.12; Ps. 2.9; Isa. 24.19; Prov. 25.19 and 18.24(?). If this is indeed an Aramaism, then Aramaisms in Hebrew are of minimal significance.

30. *sagî'*, 36.26; 34.23. See above, 4.

31. *śrh* (let loose), 37.3 and possibly Jer. 15.11. The root is certainly found in Aramaic *ś*e*rā'* and in Syriac; cf. its use in Matt. 14.23 (Pesh.) for the Greek ἀπολύω. See also Ethiopic *srh* with a *sin* (remit). Arabic *sarray* (free some one from cares), and Accadian *šāru* (open a building, dedicate). In Ugarit the meaning is 'destroy' (K I 3.6, 4.50, Gaster, Driver), a meaning which is found in Aramaic also (undo, loose, destroy). Cf. the use of the Hebrew *ḥll*, which means 'untie, loosen, make free for common use'. The word may well be a good Hebrew root, since all the transformations are normal.

Driver-Gray (*Job*, p. xlvii) give five other words which 'should also probably' be considered Aramaisms.

32. *'ekep* (pressure), 33.7 and the verb in Prov. 16.26 (urge, press). LXX did not recognize the root in 33.7 and read *kappî* (my hand), but V has *eloquentia mea* (DV, my eloquence). The idea of 'pressure, anxiety' is found in Syriac, Aramaic and Arabic. In modern Hebrew the root means both 'care, anxiety' and 'saddle' (cf. Syriac *'ōk*e*pā* and Arabic *'ikāb*). The idea of 'pressure' seems a sound enough meaning for a good Hebrew word.

33. *qtl* (kill), 13.15; 24.14; also Ps. 139.19. The root is rare in Hebrew, 'poetic and late' (*BDB*). It is found in Aramaic, Syriac, Ethiopic, Arabic, and is a perfectly good Hebrew root.

34. *šalhebet* (flame), 15.30, but see also Ezek. 21.3; Cant, 8.6. This is a good Hebrew word, being an ancient *shafel* form, *GK* 55*i*. A similar form is found in Aramaic and Syriac.

35. *rōqeb* (bottle). LXX has ἀσκός at 13.28, and so also Syriac. Cf. Arabic *raqaba* (tie by the neck). It is a good Hebrew word which LXX knew.

36. *m's* (liquify), 7.5, but there is a general consensus of opinion that the root is *mss*.

According to *BDB*, there are other Aramaisms which appear in the Book of Job.

37. *bār* (open country), 39.4; Aramaic *barā'*, Syriac *barrā'*, but also Arabic *barra*; cf. V *ad pastum*. There is no reason to doubt that it is a true Hebrew root, though rare.

38. *gēw* (midst), 30.5. According to *BDB* this is a strong Aramaism but the root is found in Arabic *gaww*. It is a rare Hebrew root, in the sense that it is found once only in the limited vocabulary of the Old Testament.

39. *gzr* (decree), 22.28. This may be an Aramaism, but it is not in the Elihu speeches. The usual meaning is 'cut, cut off, divide', Aramaic, Syriac, Ethiopic, Arabic, Ugarit. The meaning 'decree' is found only here, Esth. 2.1, the Aramaic of Daniel (4), Mishnah, Talmud and in modern Hebrew.

40. *ḥesed*, 6.14. This we understand to mean 'loyalty' as everywhere else except Lev. 20.17 H and Prov. 14.34. Hitzig and Delitzsch understand the meaning here to be 'envy, shame' as in Lev. 20.17. This is said to be an Aramaism, and it is found with this meaning as well as 'loyalty' etc. in the Targums and in Syriac but also Arabic *ḥasad*. The fact that the root with this meaning is found in Arabic suggests that it is a true general Semitic root, though rare in extant Hebrew literature. In any case, an Aramaism which appears in H suggests that, whatever 'aramaism' means, it is part of the language.

41. ḥēmāh, 36.18. Beer read this as ḥᵃmēh (beware), which is said to be an Aramaism. But even if Beer's suggestion is accepted, there is an Arabic ḥamay (protect, guard) and an Accadian ēmū (guard). Here is another rare, but truly Hebrew root.

INDEX OF NAMES

INDEX OF BIBLICAL REFERENCES
(*Except Job*)

2. 8001z